15 TO LIFE:

FROM MISFIT TO MINISTER

The Testimony of

SAMUEL DEVON JACKSON JR.

XULON
PRESS

15 to Life:
From Misfit to Minister
by Samuel Devon Jackson Jr.

Printed in the United States of America.

ISBN 9781498496568

Unless otherwise indicated, Scripture quotations taken from the King James Version (KJV) – *public domain.*

Samuel Devon Jackson Jr.
MinisterSam@outlook.com
8328743343
contact for speaking engagements

www.xulonpress.com

INTRODUCTION

This intro seems to be the hardest part of this book to write. I guess it's because I'm trying to write this over-the-top introduction. So, can I just be real with you for a minute? This book comes from a man who has been through some pretty tough times. Yes, I know we've all been through something and yes, we've all dealt with our issues on different levels. However, I just want to share with you what I believe God has shown me to share with you.

My background isn't much different from many of you, and I pray this book reaches those f you who may have family members and or have been through similar tough times. I come from one of the worst parts of Houston, TX, known as Fifth Ward. This area was known for killings, robberies and all types of criminal activity. And yes, I got caught up in some of those criminal activities. I did the crimes and yes I did the time.

However, this book is about the life and the events that helped shape me into the man I am today. Sometimes in life we have to go through something in order to be who God has called us to be. So if you will, join me on this journey as we see how God takes a young man of the streets and transforms him into the man of God he is today.

TABLE OF CONTENTS

MISFIT TO MINISTER

Written especially for Samuel Jackson

*Somewhere it can be read what your life
had in store,
Maybe a path of destruction at the open
of every door.
As a misfit, I'm sure your life was riding
on a rail,
For you laid down your own path, a
road straight to hell.
Once having a life of sin that you chose
to live,
You would soon realize just how little
you had to give.
I can't really say for sure for I did not
know you back then,*

But I'm honored to know you now and
you are not going back there again.
With a tap on your shoulder one day you
heard a voice so stern and true,
You've tried it on your own and failed,
so today let me help you.
Now you're a changed man and became
a minister for all to see,
Touching the lives of many, yes
including me.
Doing God's work and now reaching for
the sky's brightest star,
Not looking back since you've raised
the bar.
Allowing our true father to make you a
new path, one much better than before,
At the end of the day I'm sure God isn't
the only one keeping score.
There's a bible to be read, notes to be
kept, prayers to be said,
Thanks and praise to be given and
fulfilling God's purpose all before
going to bed.
You wake the next morning thanking
God as you put your feet on the floor,

*You see a promising day and you're now
blessed when you open the door.
The God you once failed is the same that
has forgiven you,
So you can bring light to others just as
you so often do.
Keep reaching for the stars and you'll
soon see it's true,
That we are all blessed just because of
knowing you.
Author: Lisa Paulich*

ACKNOWLEDGMENTS

First and foremost, I want to thank my Lord Jesus Christ for loving me when I was unlovable and giving His life for me.

I want to thank my mother Dorothy R. Carrethers who loved and cared for me no matter what I did. Who stood by me when no one else did and was so understanding and patient even when I was unbearable!

Also to my grandparents both sides and my Uncle Daryl and Aunt Merlyn who took care of me and tried to raise me in the right way. It took a while but I got it.

To my Uncle Donald and Uncle Charles and their wives you made life interesting. Love you!

To Chaplain Hart who took a young man and raised him into a God-fearing man. Not just a Godly man but also a natural man, you taught me so much.

To Pastor Keenan Smith, your leadership and your love for God's people is truly amazing!

To my brothers: Chris (Mak) Jackson, Brian (Beto) Jackson, Corey Sheldon Miles and Quinten Jackson (Cousin/lil brother). I love you guys so much.

And my sisters: Lekevia, Jamie, Theresa, Paula and Stacia (Cousin/lil sister) you guys are something fierce...I love you guys.

And to Sandra K, what can I say, you are the best step-mom in the world.

And saving the best for last, my best friend, my soulmate, my wife Mrs. Tera I Jackson. I praise God for you because you make me want to do better in life. You show me so much love even when you don't have to. We've been through some rough times but you have never wavered in standing by me. You encourage me when I'm down and you build me up when I'm weak. I thank you so much for being who you are.

To Mr. and Mrs. Jimmy and Ethel Hall, for your unfailing love, support and understanding. You were there through thick and thin. I thank you so much for all that you've done. The best in-laws a man can have. I love you so much!

And last of all, to those people who have played vital parts in my past. Thank you for the roles you played in my life whether good or bad. You too have helped shape me into the man I am today. You all have given me something to build upon, from having been in my life. May God bless you always!

PREFACE

15 to Life, From Misfit to Minister, is a book that's being written to open the eyes of those who may be struggling in areas that for some reason they feel they have no hope. In this book, I want to share my struggles but also my triumphs. I want the reader to know that in a world of hopelessness, there is hope! And that no matter how bad things may look, things do get better if your hope is in Jesus Christ and His saving Grace.

15 to Life, is about how during my 15 years of incarceration God transformed a thug in the streets into a man of God. Those years made me take a good long look at myself for who I truly was. And how having truly lost myself I found myself. My hope is that through my story others will be inspired to lean into the things of God and trust that HE has more instore for their lives than they can ever imagine.

SPECIAL THANKS

I want to extend a special thanks to Mrs. Rachel Butler for taking on the responsibility of editing 15 to Life. Your words of encouragement helped me out of some tough spots. Words alone cannot express the gratitude that I have for you. You are truly a blessing! Thank you so much!

To my church family, Crosby Church you are amazing! Every time I stepped foot in the church, I was asked, "How's the book coming?" That alone let me know that you cared and wanted to see my success. I love you dearly. Thank You!

And to my niece Shaundraya (Pye'nu) Oliver, your perseverance is on a level all by itself. You are the strongest young lady that I know and your heart is so filled with love. Thank you for being who you are!

And again, to my lovely wife, what can I say you are AWESOME! I love you so much! I thank you from the bottom of my heart for being patient with me while writing this book. Your emotional support has been outstanding. I praise God for you!

To my writing team at Xulon Press you guys are awesome! May God, bless you in all that you do. Thank you so much!

Chapter 1

EARLY MEMORIES

Wow! As I think back over my earlier years it really amazes' me of how my earliest memories are from the tender years of about two to maybe four years old. As I ponder over what those times were like, it brings up memories that I haven't thought about in years. Memories of joy and pain, and memories of achievements and disappointments.

The thoughts that are running through my head right now are overwhelming! As I reflect on my life and try to sort out everything it tends to get a little stressful. As I'm sitting with my mom, I've decided that I might as well pick her brain for a little information. I'm just glad I'm doing it now due to her battle with onset Alzheimer's. Plus, it brings up bad memories of bad times, and how we suffered just to get by.

Thinking back on those memories I can remember our family doing a lot of moving from Houston to Oklahoma to Denton and back. My memories are pretty much about going up and down the highways with my face plastered to the car window and just enjoying the life of a toddler. I can see it as plain as if it were yesterday, on the road looking at all the nice cars and the amazing sceneries and meeting all the wonderful people at the different stops. However, as I think back I always wondered why we were moving so much. But at this young age for any child, the number one question is always "why?" in regards to everything.

I can remember one day during the summer at my grandparent's house in Oklahoma City, OK. I believe I was about two years old at the time, I was outside trying to climb a tree, just being an average little boy. As I was climbing the tree and reaching heights that I had never experienced before as a two-year-old, I was focusing on each branch and where I would place each hand. As I reached for the next branch I felt this painful prick in my right thumb. Without thinking I snatched my hand back, forgetting all about being in a tree and down I went. I would have to say looking back it probably was about 5 to 6 feet that I was up in that tree. But to a two-year-old that might as well have been 10 to 12 feet. Once I hit the ground all I can remember is screaming at the top of my lungs and my mom running out to see what was going on. When she got to me all I heard was, "Oh my God what's wrong with my baby!" My arm began to change colors and to swell by the minute. So, my mom got my grandparents and they put me into the car and we took off to the hospital. When we arrived at the hospital the doctor informed my mother that if we had been a few minutes late I would have died due to a Brown Recluse spider bite. This was my first encounter with death but it wouldn't be my last.

As my mind drifts, back and forth I can't help but remember a time in Denton, Texas when my uncle and older cousin had me and my brother fight each other. And yes, I did say fight as in punching and wrestling. We were in the living room and as I recall they were relaxing a little. That's code for drinking. This was the first time that my brother and I fought, but it wouldn't be our last. After our little bout, they waged a little tickle war on my brother and me. It was on this day that I believe I also began to stutter, while I'm thinking about it.

The more I think about it the more that I am sure that this is when the stuttering started, because I can't remember anytime that I stuttered before then. This stuttering would haunt me all my elementary years, because kids can and will be very cruel. In the beginning, I was taunted and mocked to the point that it helped to fuel an anger that was already growing. So, instead of getting bullied, I became the bully, because of the shame. The stuttering was a very tough time for me it made me very self-conscious and shy.

After settling into our new home things began to change. My uncle and cousin left and it was just the family:

mom, dad, my two brothers and me. Our family dynamic didn't get bad all at once, it kind of took a slow decline. My dad was working at one time, but somehow that ended swiftly, and my mother was the breadwinner in the home. We hardly ever saw mom, the reason being she was always at work and when she did come home it was our bedtime. But she would always make sure that we were alright. My father on the other hand, for some reason always had his own thing going on, what that was, I have no idea. We began to see groups of guys come over to the house for long periods of time and they would do a lot of smoking and drinking. Our home quickly became a hangout for drug use and partying. Mom would have to come home and take care of us because we were being neglected because our dad wanted to have his fun all day.

I guess the time era for all of this would be around 1976 or 1977 and I believe this was in Oklahoma City, Oklahoma. I believe the house was white and it had a fenced in backyard. And it was in a pretty good neighborhood, but again I was just a little boy. It was at this time or shall I say, it was at this stage in my life that everything changed.

I can remember a time I tried to make us breakfast. My little brothers had gotten hungry and our daddy was passed out on the sofa. I tried to wake him, but all he did was sit up half way and immediately sunk back into the sofa. And as I began to walk off, I happened to look down and saw drugs and liquor all over the floor by the sofa. So being the big brother I took it upon myself to try and make breakfast for me and my little brothers. I believe I made them eggs, bacon, and toast, but for some strange reason everything turned out black.

The smoke that went throughout the house woke my father, and it set him into a drunken frenzy. He began cursing and fussing until he got to me, as he began to whoop me, I couldn't understand why he was so mad, all I was trying to do was feed my little brothers and make sure that they were alright. After he calmed down from his drunken fit it seemed as if he just went back to sleep. But by that time, we were confined to our room and made to lay down.

As time moved on, we were still hungry so we decided that we would walk to Robertson Grocery store. Mr. and Mrs. Robertson owned the neighborhood store and Mrs. Robertson took a liking to us. She missed her grandchildren because they lived so far away and they didn't visit much. So, she took us to her house and fed us and let us watch a little television. Meanwhile, her husband called our mom at work to let her know that her children were at their house and that she could come get us when she got off.

By the time mom got off work our father had gotten to a point of drunkenness that I will never forget. That night when our mother got home our father was in a rage like never before, he began to cuss and fuss and got very violent. He went about slamming doors and knocking over objects in the house. He was calling us all kind of names and telling us that he was about to kill us. Now mind you this is a PK (Preacher's Kid)! But this is what happens when the streets get a hold of you. And so, my mom finally got a chance to get away from him and she called his parents and told them that if they wanted their son they'd better come and get him.

So, after a few hours, my uncle Daryl comes over just to find that his brother has left the house. So, my uncle hung around for a few minutes, just to make sure that everything was all right. This was the first of many times that my uncle would have to come by our house. He truly stepped up for us. This was the most horrific time that I can remember.

Now, my father was not all bad. He tried in some areas but his bad outweighed his good. During this time, I believe we were in Oklahoma City and we stayed down the street from the State Capitol. As time went, things got worse, my father and my mom's fights went from the verbal to the physical and I can remember one fight where my mom and dad were getting into it and my brother tried to stop them from fighting and he grabbed my father's leg and was yelling for him to stop. My father was so upset that he flung my little brother by his leg into their large dresser hurting my brothers back.

As my brother began to yell and cry my mother raced to defend my little brother and my father slammed her face into our glass table, pushing her bottom teeth up through her bottom lip. I believe this fight lasted a few hours and somehow my mom found a way to once again, to call my uncle. When my uncle arrived, my mom begged my uncle to get my father out of the house before someone gets killed. This was the official beginning of the end, it was the kickoff of the destruction of our family.

As the years went on, times at home began to get worse. My father would often come home from hanging out with his friends and he would be so high from the drugs that he'd been smoking all day, that in his mind everybody in our house was out to get him. I think during these times I must have been about three or four years old. Anyway, he would come in slamming doors and cursing out my mom for no reason at all. Now mind you, my mom has been at work all day and my father hadn't, but he didn't care!

So, he begins to manhandle my mom and the fighting begins. My mom somehow manages to get away and she gets us and hides us in the closet. However, I always managed to see what was going on. He was slapping and throwing my mom all around the house. All the while I'm thinking why is this happening? Why does he hate us so much? What did we do to him? I would have to say that these years were the worse because these times seemed like a nightmare.

As I stated earlier, there were some alright times. And what I mean by alright is, even when my dad tried to be ok there would always be some kind of accident that would happen. Like there was this one time we went to Six Flags, my brothers and I were so excited when we pulled into the parking lot. The huge rides just amazed us! As we were getting out of the car I reached to get out and as my hand was outside of the car, my dad slammed the car door on my hand. And no I don't think he did it on purpose but that's how things seemed to always happen. And through all of that, we still managed to enjoy our day at Six Flags even with my hand hurting. But anyway, we had the time of our lives. As the day came to a close and we were heading to the car my dad was putting things into the trunk and me wanting to see what my dad was doing I had my little hands on the bottom part of the trunk and as you would have it my hands got slammed in the trunk. So, yes that's twice in one day. So, see even when not trying, things always happened.

As life moved on, things began to change within our household dynamics.

My mother and father began to really go their separate ways. Our family was being destroyed by all the drinking and drugging that my father was doing. It seemed that the city life had taken what was once a country preacher's kid, and changed him into a monster. But I have to give it to mom, she tried! My grandmother would often talk with her about hanging in there because divorce was not allowed in the Church of Christ.

However, things weren't getting any better, in fact, things were getting worse, our father was getting more violent. On any given night, we didn't know whether we were going to live or die. This was a scary time for our family! A mom and three little boys can really do nothing against a grown man who is amped up on drugs. Remember, this is the mid 70's and dope heads were crazy back then, plus you have to remember my father was a country boy and on top of that he was a preacher's kid. So, when my father moved to Houston, the city life took him kind of fast.

During this time my only job was to watch over my little brothers and make sure that they were safe. It was a job that I gladly accepted. Our lives were like a roller coaster, we never knew what was about to happen next. All we knew was that our mom was always working and our father was always getting high. He was so gone off the drugs, that I can remember a time when my mom gave him an ultimatum. She told him that it was either the drugs or your three boys! He paused for a minute and then chose the drugs.

The next phase of my memories is in Houston, Texas. I believe the year is around 1977 or 78. And let's see, that should make me around 5 or 6 years old and the little man of the house. During this time, I asked if I could go and stay with my mom's parents. My granny had just had a stroke and it scared the life out of me. I can remember going to the bathroom and the door wouldn't open, I pushed and I pushed, but it just wouldn't budge. I screamed for my mom to come open the door because I had to go really bad. My mom got the door cracked a little and she happened to see my grandmother lying on the floor leaning against the bathroom door. Upon seeing that, my mom began to yell at the top of her lungs for her daddy. While my grandfather was trying to get, the door open my mother called for emergency assistance. This was a very scary time for a little kid to have to go through. I can't remember how long my granny stayed in the hospital all I know is after she was released I wanted to go back to Houston with her and that's just what I did.

After arriving in Houston with my granny, I began looking after her the best I could. I would make sure she was getting rest and I would help her out around the house and the yard. During this time, she was also helping to raise my little cousin and I would watch as she would bathe her in the kitchen sink. I would often be scared that she would go down the drain of the sink, because she was so tiny. It's funny how we think at such a young age. My cousin and I would sit on the floor in the afternoons and watch our favorite cartoon, "Popeye the sailor man". She would come running to me screaming, "Popeye the man, is coming on! Come on!" I enjoyed this time in my life because it was safe. It was just me, my little cousin and my grandparents and it was awesome.

As the months moved on it was getting closer to the time for me to start school. I can remember the first day as I left my grandparents yard and got on the bus, really it was a station wagon.

But that's neither here nor there. I can remember feeling very sad that I was leaving my granny and papa for the first time. I can still see the inside of the station wagon all those little kids spread out in the back of that little wagon. These memories I tend to cherish because this was when my life begin to really change for the better.

No more watching my father trip out on my mom and no more feeling scared. The elementary school that I went to was pretty good they really cared for their kids. But still, I missed my granny and papa I was missing my papa time. My papa and I would sit and watch cowboy shows all day. We would start with Rawhide and end the day with Gun Smoke. Man! I truly miss those days!

As I sit and think back on those days, I can't help but feel a certain way. At this time in my life, my little mind is going back and forth. From my mom and brothers who had moved back to Houston to my grandparents and little cousin. I was getting home sick as every day went by. During this time, life seemed to be pretty good, there was no more abuse in the home. I believe this is when my father began to become a figment of my imagination.

Living on Green St., was a true learning experience, we had this neighbor who had a gang of dogs and when I would walk by her house the smell would dang near knock me out.

Now, remember this was the 70's and times were hard for everybody. But for a single parent especially a black woman with three young boys, it was dang near impossible to get by. I remember trips down to the record shop with mom, just her and her three boys, and then getting home and mom trying to teach us how to dance. I think the worm or the snake was out then and to reflect back on that, is pretty funny.

Mom would come home and play with us a little and then ask us to dance with her. Mom kept us focused on the happy things instead of what was really around us. As I look back I can honestly say I really didn't know that we were poor. And that's because mom hid it from us. Mom would take us out walking and for some reason, we always had trash bags with us and mom would challenge us to see who could get the most aluminum cans in their bags. My brothers and I just thought we were racing each other but the truth was that we were poor and that we needed the extra money. Mom was great, after our outings we would come home and mom would fix our food and then she would go and lay down because she said she was tired. But come to find out she went to bed because that was all we had and she would often go hungry in order to feed us. That's the type of mom I have!

During the late 70's I began to experience the realness of life. Mom had arranged for this young man to come by and babysit us for a few hours and he would put on this fake face while she was around, but as soon as she left, OH MY GOD! He would terrorize me, I would cry for hours and he would drive me crazy. This was my first encounter of being bullied. And it was terror!

The only male role model during this time was my grandfather, my mom's dad. He was a man that loved to tell stories and he could tell some good ones. I remember he would say some things that even until this day I still don't understand. Here's one: "Up the gum tree down the pine, split my britches from behind." Till this very day, I have no clue what that means. But there are some sayings that the light bulb has come on. Like, "Never let anyone stay in your mind rent free!" Which to me means you have to forgive others because if you don't they hold power over you and they don't even know it. Here's another, "Can't catch a canary bird in a wrestling jacket." WHAT! He would come over and make us rice and sausage and it was the best meal a kid could have because it was from pawpaw. As I think about those times I can remember how he would spend most of his day with us, just sitting out on the porch with us telling us stories. These are the memories I will always cherish.

Now I can't talk about my grandfather without mentioning my grandmother. She was a pistol; she was the most headstrong woman I ever knew.

She wouldn't waste any time getting on to you if you were acting up, she was the quickest grandmother I ever saw. I can remember a time when my brothers, my little cousin, and I went to the Post Office with her and we were running all over the place just being kids. Then all of a sudden, she yelled out, "stop running, be still and sit down!" Now my little brother, my cousin and I stopped dead in our tracks, but my middle brother got caught. She popped him so hard that she left her palm print on his thigh. That scared the mess out of us. We got so quiet that you could hear a pin drop. After we left the Post Office, we went back home and she fixed us all a little snack. She acted as if nothing ever happened, but we were still in shock

about the hand print on my brothers'
leg. That was a bad pop on the leg!

My grandmother wasn't a force to be
reckoned with, only standing about five
feet tall, she didn't take any mess. I can
remember her working in her garden,
digging around on her hands and knees
and just sweating away. So, I decided to
make her a tool that would allow her to
not have to stoop down so much. So, I
took her garden shovel and a long stick
and nailed them together and she kept
that tool until she died. I remember my
granny killing a possum with that tool,
and when she would stab at the possum
she would grit her teeth. In fact, whenever she would do just about anything
and she was focused on it, she would
grit her teeth. She would teach us how

to clean up and was serious about it. She was so thorough that it would drive you crazy. But you knew she loved you and you couldn't help but to love her.

My grandparents were some very special people; they would often step in to help my mother out with us. And when I say often I really mean most of the time. They were more so, our stand by parents. I believe my cleaning fits come from my grandmother and the little earthly wisdom that I do have besides coming from God my grandfather helped me with that. I wish everyone in the world could have met them!

Thinking back over my earlier years I had a lot of guidance. Both sets of grandparents tried to direct me in the right direction, but I was too blind to actually see it. The grandparents I just talked about were my mother's parents and they were something else. You talk about opposites attract! They were like night and day. Actually, I always felt that my grandparents on both sides should have been switched. My mom's mom should have been married to my father's father and my mom's father should have been married to my father's mom. Because to me, that matched. But, God saw otherwise.

I remember when we stayed on Sumpter St. it was a pretty good house and we were doing ok. I had begun to make friends and life started to feel good. On the way to school I would often stop off at my best friend's house and we would watch "Yo MTV Raps" before we had to take off for school. But on the way to school, we would stop by another friend's house and then we would head on out to school. We would laugh all the way. It was just me, Andre and David. David was crazy he would call himself, Big D. He was always funny. Andre, on the other hand, was a natural born entertainer, every year he would win the Michael Jackson dance off. Man! Andre had all the moves down, he was a natural. But for some reason, those times moved on pretty fast.

As the years moved on the group of friends began to change. I began to hang around the house and kick it with the kids on my block and this is when the anger inside of me began to show its ugly head. I would get into fights and do some of the craziest things. I remember one time I tried to smash this one kid with his own bicycle and one of the girls in the neighborhood ran to get my mom and she was the only one who could have stopped me. I hate to say it but truly this was more than anger it was more on the side of rage I would get so angry that I would begin to cry and then everything would just go blank. A new way of life had begun to show its ugly head.

Chapter 2

CALL OF THE STREETS

I t's now 1983 and my life's about to take a serious turn. Hurricane Alicia has just passed through. And I guess hurricane Alicia must have had more meaning for me than I could have ever imagined. Now for those who can remember hurricane Alicia, remembers the destruction she brought to Texas and how she put Houston on its butt. Now I'm not saying I was tearing things up and that I was this big bad guy. However, I was headed on a path of destruction that would lead me down some pretty dark roads. Roads that would take me to hell and back. And come to think of it, I did uproot myself from the real things that mattered and latched onto the lies of the devil.

Once I stopped hanging out with my elementary friends, my life changed. The other kids on my block, was where I gravitated to, the ones who stayed in trouble. Why I don't know! I began to stay out late and found myself always being tested. Back then kids wanted to see if you could fight and if you were down for the hood. And my hood was known as "Tha Bloody Nickle" or "Fifth Ward." Now believe me when I tell you, I didn't have any problems with fighting!

55

My saying use to be, "Win, lose, or draw! Let's get it!" That was my attitude, that's who I felt I had to be at the time. Sorry, but it's the truth!

I would do some of the craziest things during this phase of my life. I would talk about other kids so bad that it would make them want to fight. And to be honest about it that was what I wanted, for you to want to fight. There was this one time that we were playing basketball in our backyard and this kid was talking smack. I took the basketball and just launched it at his face. And after it connected I just starting hitting him until he started bleeding. It was like I just blacked out, I couldn't see anything but him and me hurting him. My mom had to come get me off of him and drag me into the house. She would yell at me at the top of her lungs, "Boy! What is wrong with you? Are you crazy?" I would just sit there mad, mad at the world. And I didn't even know why.

As time moved on, we moved from Sumpter St. to Green St. and we moved right next door to my grandparents. This is when it really got bad, the call of the streets began to get louder and louder. Where we stayed was right down the street from one of the most ruthless projects in Houston known as the Kelly Courts. Going into these projects you had to know how to fight or you were going to get beat up every day. And the kids from Kelly Courts could fight! So you either stayed out or you learned to fight really quick. I went in a couple of times but I soon found out I was no match for these kids. They had styles of fighting and at this time I had no style, I just fought. So I hung around my block and made friends with the kids on my block.

By this time, I was just starting middle school and as everyone knows going from elementary school to middle school is a huge transition. I can remember my first day it was like being in a different world. I saw teachers in a whole new light. These teachers were young and attractive; some actually could have been models. And my homeroom teacher she was a knockout! But once the bell rang for the first-period class it seemed like everything changed again.

Going into those hallways was like entering a war zone. Some of the kids I knew and some I'd never seen before. Lunch time was a free for all, the older kids would pick on the younger ones and the larger kids would terrorize the smaller ones. I kind of fit somewhere in the middle, plus I knew a few people. But that didn't stop the ones who didn't know me. Some of them would bump you on the stairs just to see what you would do. If you didn't say anything you were considered weak and you were placed at the bottom of the food chain. But if you spoke out they would try you to see just how far you would go. You really just had to pick and choose your battles. Some I misjudged and was called out to fight after school. The battleground for the fights was in a funeral home parking lot. And you better had shown up or you would be called out every day until you did. I thought I was tough, but I had nothing on those kids.

During the summer of my sixth-grade year, things went a little crazy. After seeing girls in a new light and my interest being peaked. I was introduced to pornography by some friends and this opened up a whole new world for me. Some of my friends and I would get together and look at dirty magazines and x rated films all day long. I can only speak for myself, but I would be mesmerized by what I saw.

Little did I know what was in store for me because of porn. Anyway, this must have lasted the majority of the summer. But right towards the end of the summer, something happened that would change me forever.

I was headed down to Tyrone's house another one of my good friends, and his neighbor Mr. Dan came out. I think I may have been 12 or 13 years old at the time. Anyway, he began to ask me questions, like do you like to read magazines? If so, what kinds? Of course, I said yes thinking I was going to get something for free. Little did I know the cost would be priceless. Because what I was about to pay, there are no refunds. So, he told me that he had some magazines that he thought

I'd like. As he motioned me over I had an uncomfortable feeling but for some reason, I didn't pay it any attention. So, I went in and he told me to have a seat on the couch while he went and got the magazines. As I sat there waiting, he came out of his bedroom with a brown paper sack and throws it in my lap. He tells me, "this is just between me and you, okay!" Not thinking much of it, I just shrugged my shoulders and said, "ok"! As I open the bag, low and behold I saw all kinds of nude magazines. He tells me to go ahead and check them out. So being the inquisitive young boy that I was, I did!

As I began looking and not turning away, I began to get excited and Mr. Dan noticed. He began to put his hands on me and tells me, "its ok, don't be ashamed it's natural." So, he just kept rubbing me, until he made his way to my genital area. By this time, I was scared half to death and I didn't know what to do. He began to sense my fear and gently whispered, "you'd better not tell anyone or I will kill your whole family and it will be all your fault!" After he whispered this, he unzipped my pants and began to molest me and I just started to cry. I was so scared! I didn't know what to think about myself, for one I couldn't believe that this was happening. Why me?! Why me?!

After the Mr. Dan tragedy, I would never be the same. My attitude was already terrible, but now it was off the charts. I just didn't care. I was hurt so now I really wanted to hurt others. No matter the cost! I started chasing girls like never before. I would tell them whatever they wanted to hear just to get what I wanted. And then it was on to the next female and I mean, I would just up and disappear and wouldn't look back.

I'm now mid-way into my seventh-grade year and I have this attitude, that I will do whatever I want and no one can tell me different. By now I had made some different friends and we formed a little clique. We did everything together, hang out in the hall, hang out at lunch time, even if we didn't have the same lunch period we found a way to be together. We even cut class together. These were my defiant years, the years in which I was so called smelling myself.

My friends and I would skip school like every other day and hang out at Kevin's house, one of my good friends and do all kinds of stuff. We were some real misfits; we would eat like kings at Kevin's house because he had an uncle who worked for Jack-in-the-box. And from time to time we would get some girls to come over to have some fun and just kick it. As much as I hate to say it, this was the beginning of my woman-izing phase. And I think this is where I first tried my first cigarette and first beer. We thought we were the stuff.

After school was a whole new ball game! The kids in my neighborhood were pretty out there. My middle brother, Chris and I would often go around the corner to our friends' house to play some basketball, kick-ball, baseball and catch in their yard. I can remember one year I think it was the summer of 1985 and we were headed around the corner to play. And my friends had gotten some new neighbors it was a house full of young black males and they were real kool. They had new cars and they wore a lot of jewelry, and on their porch, were a sea of brand new, brand name sneakers. And their clothes were top of the line! They had the most popular sweat suits like Adidas and Nike. Some of these guys even had a few gold teeth. And the girls that would stop by, they were gorgeous!

Seeing all this had me sold, this is what I wanted! So now I had to see what was going on and how they were getting all this stuff. And I soon found out really quick, what was going on! It seemed like what was going on was an all-day affair. Where there would be all sorts of people coming to their house like clockwork. I remember one time I saw one of the guys hand this other guy a small baggie and it had what appeared to be a small yellowish crumb in it. All I know is the guy he handed it too was very excited. I think I may have watched this for about 2 to 3 months. And I realized that these guys were making a grip of money. So naturally I wanted in, but it wasn't that easy. Some of the guys wouldn't even talk about it. But in the hood, you had to learn by watching, not by talking.

I can remember when I first started getting into the streets. Since the guys at the house across the street from my homeboys wouldn't teach us anything. My middle brother and I would go and hang out in the Kelly Courts which was right down the street from our house. We started out just playing basketball and kicking it with a few friends. As a matter of fact, this is also when I learned how to play basketball, which by the way I became pretty good at. Our squad owned the court, not bragging now! Just saying!

However, life quickly changed from playing basketball to running the streets. I can remember the first time that dope was put into my hands. By dope I mean crack cocaine. I was told to bring back $100.00 on a sack that was worth $350.00 which would allow me to get myself started out. This was done by a friend of mine who had gotten his start because of his big brother. It's like I said, getting started in this line of business was a hard thing to do. Mainly because of the high risk of being robbed, going to prison, or even getting killed. And all of this could happen just by someone opening their mouth and telling the wrong person. But once you're in, you're in and it is a life like no other.

In the first couple of years of me trying to sell drugs, I didn't make any profit. One thing you come to understand, the dope game gives you an upper hand with women who are hooked on this stuff, they will do ANYTHING to get it. And if you have what they want, then they will do anything for you to get it. And being a teenager at the time with my hormones running wild I would use this drug to have the times of my life. For almost two to three years I never saw any profit, in fact, I would have to think of other ways like robbing to get my money to buy more drugs to sell. And this was a whole other life.

During these years, I felt that I was living a players dream. Meaning you could have some of the finest women do whatever you wanted. Now the trick in this was, you had to get a dope user and not a dope head. A dope user is a person who still has enough care for themselves that they try to keep themselves up. And a dope head just doesn't care! They just want their next fix. The dope users would be mothers, college girls, and business women, but you would have to catch them tweaking. And when they were tweaking they would do anything for you, just to get their next high. Crack would make people do some of worst things, things that they would never do, to or with other people.

As time went on, and I began to understand more and more of the streets. Things began to change in a way that was unheard of, crack changed people for the worst. It turned ordinary mothers into streetwalkers and top notch athletes into either drug lords or dope heads. To see people, you know go from stars to zombies was crazy. One minute they're upbeat and the next they're down and out. Seeing this really made an impact on me. Even though I was in the drug game I made myself a promise that I would never try crack cocaine. I did weed and I would drink I even had embalming fluid slipped on me once. But crack, no way! I can remember seeing some of my friend's moms on the streets trying to find a fix and from that point on I decided I would never sell to any of my friends' moms. As a matter of fact, my home-boys and I made a pact that we would never sell to one another's mother.

During this phase of my life, I was getting really out of control. My mom was always working and her parents were doing their best to help raise us, but I was getting out there. I was getting into fights like clockwork. I was truly on a dark path and I was fading fast. I went through so much during this time that drinking and getting high was my only way of dealing. I can remember times when one of my good friends would come by first thing in the morning and he would just drop a $25-dollar bag of weed on my chest and tell me, "let's get the day started!" This would begin my day and it wouldn't stop until I went to sleep the next day.

During these times I would get into all kinds of trouble. At this time in my life, I had quit school and was just hanging out. Doing nothing with my life! I felt like or shall I say my mindset was, tomorrow isn't promised so I might as well get the most out of today. During this time in my life I wondered about aimlessly, no direction what so ever. All I wanted to do was mess with girls, smoke weed and drink beer. Nothing was more important at the time, NOTHING!

As I think back on these times I had quit going to church and I didn't have any connection with God what so ever. I believe I quit going because I felt like an outcast. The church my family attended at this time was all about fashion and we were poor, so we didn't fit in. So, I felt that I didn't need to put up with that so I just stopped going. And I just started living for myself. In essence, the streets became my family. I was worshipping my flesh and trying to serve it with everything that I had. Don't get me wrong I believed that there was a God and I believed in Jesus Christ. But I didn't know them and wasn't trying to get to know them during this particular time either.

During this time in my life, I was trying to live my life as a thug and getting pretty good at it. I was hanging with known thugs and was fitting in and was getting a little bit of status too. I had begun to develop a taste for firearms and it was serious. My homeboys and I would go to pawn shops and check out what types of merchandise they had, but I would go straight to the guns and I would be in a daze as to all the nice guns that they had. But for some reason, we never had the chance to rob them. We would always plan to, but it would never happen. Why? I don't know! The only thing I can come up with is that God had His hand on me. Didn't know it then, though!

During this phase in my life, I had the idea that I was this crazy thug who would do anything to come up. No matter how dangerous! I can remember a time when a few friends and I were planning this lick (i.e. robbery), and I had made up my mind that if it came to it, I would engage the police in a shoot-out. But now as I look back, I thank God that this never happened.

My mind was in a very dangerous place; I didn't care about anything or anyone. And to be honest I wasn't raised that way, so I don't know where that line of thinking came from. I was actually raised in the church, but never got anything out of it.

As the years went on I was getting a little name for myself. I was getting known in the Kelly Courts and in the juke joint down the street. I was starting to make a little money in the drug game and I mean a little. I was barely making a profit, but it beat not having money. My play sister Pebbles would even let me chill at her apartment and take care of my business. Life was good! But it was a life without God, I was truly serving the devil, not in a direct sense but in an indirect sense. I stopped going to church and nothing I did had God in it, life was about feeding my flesh. And I tried to feed it until it burst!

As I walked in this lifestyle, I began to move around Houston on a regular basis. I would hang out in Lakewood, Sunnyside, and Southpark, just to name a few places. My theme became, "Papa was a rolling stone, wherever he laid his hat was his home!" Womanizing was my thing I just couldn't help it. I would probably be at my mom's house maybe 5 to 6 times out of a year. This street life was something else, there were no rules. It was get it, how you get it!

I can remember this one occasion when I went home my friends who stayed around the corner came by and asked me to come around and talk to their brother-in-law and his best friend. So, I went and we immediately hit it off. We sat down and talked about how they could make a little extra money from their military checks that they were receiving on a monthly basis. I spouted out a few ideas, some they liked and some were too risky. So, they invited me down to Killeen, Texas to spend a few days with them and meet some people. I agreed and we left about a few days later.

Going to Killeen was a whole new ball game, it was mind blowing. I was introduced to all kinds of women and they were wild. I had a different girl every night and they were ok with it. My boys had wives so they just chilled and let me do my thang. I remember the first night I was there and the girls wanted to smoke weed. Nobody knew how to roll weed except me, so I went into the bedroom and about four or five women followed me in. They were asking me all types of questions and seemed to be intrigued at the answers I was giving them. Anyway, a few of the women began to flirt with me, telling me what all they would and could do to me. I mean it was crazy!

I think I stayed in Killeen for about a month and the guys and I grew very close. We became more like brothers, especially Guy he was more of a big brother to me. We would horseplay like we had been knowing each other our whole lives. He taught me a whole lot about life and how to have fun. Pat was more about his family because he had just had a little girl. And he was always on the go. So, that left me and Guy either going over to his house to chill with his family and he had a wonderful family they were the nicest people you could ever meet. These were some memorable times for me.

Then came time for me to go back to Houston for a bit. I had to arrange some business there to take back to Killeen. So, I went back and began to put things in motion. But things were moving a bit slow and it was getting frustrating. Because I was ready to get back to Killeen it was fun there and I was missing the place. But things weren't happening the way or shall I say they weren't happening at the speed that I preferred. So I waited and waited and waited. It seemed like forever!

Chapter 3

THE LOSS OF A FRIEND

As the days went by and the days turned into weeks, I had convinced a few friends to come back with me. We were excited about the events that were about to take place. During my time in Killeen, I had managed to get hooked up with a Puerto Rican who wanted to start moving kilos of cocaine into Houston for $20,000 a bird. I managed to make a few connections and was on my way to the big leagues. And

I was ready, I had my crew and had the hookup and I had the supplier. Just needed to get back and lock everything in.

I rounded up the guys and we set out for our trip. It seemed that everybody wanted to go by their girls' house and say they're goodbyes. So, I went by my girlfriends' house and we talked about me leaving and what was about to go down. It was something strange about that night, it was like it was in slow motion. We argued and fussed about me doing something better with my life, but at this stage in my life, I just couldn't see it.

So, we went outside and sat on the steps and she talked some more about better possibilities. But I wasn't trying to hear it. It was getting late and we needed to hit the road. So, I rounded up the guys and we started to head out. We just had one more stop. We stopped by Wheatley Plaza because one of the guys needed to grab somethings. So, we jumped out and for some reason, this old man told us to be careful and to not get into any trouble. We kind of blew him off and headed inside the apartment. We were so messed up off drugs that we couldn't focus. When we came out to hit the road the old man was slump down on the driver side with a bullet hole in his head. I couldn't believe it, we had just spoken to the old man. So, we hurried to the car and headed out. But like I said we were messed up and kind of numb to what was going on.

As we were on our way, we began to talk about what had just happened and if we had stayed out there just a little while longer there wasn't no telling what would have happened. That could have been one of us, there was just no telling. But that thought didn't last long because we hurried up and fired up more weed and we just smoked and smoked. The car looked like there was a cloud from the sky inside. As we were on the road things began to get a little hazy.

I think I must have fallen asleep because the next thing I remembered was hearing the tires on the bumps that are on the shoulder of the highway. I looked over and my homeboy was knocked out, sound asleep. I screamed at him to wake him and made him pull over letting him know that he could have killed us. So, I jumped into the driver's seat and took over the drive. I turned up the music and rolled down the windows and took off. We were having a good time talking about the events that were about to take place. And how we were about to come up in the dope game.

Then suddenly I heard the same thing I heard when my homeboy fell asleep the thud of the tires rolling over the bumps on the shoulder. And I realized that I had fallen asleep it scared me to death. I could have killed us! So, I pulled over and got out of the car just to get some air, it was twice we had just had a brush with death. But to be honest I was numb to what was going on I just knew we had to get to Killeen. That was the goal!

As we continued our trip, we began planning our strategy as to how we wanted things to go. We were going to supply the Kelly Courts and the Bottoms with kilos and some of the other areas we knew about in the greater Houston area. As we got closer to Killeen I began to get the guys to get themselves together, because it was about business now. The things we had to discuss was the most serious of matters. It involved some real cut throat fellows and at this level screw ups and stupidity are not allowed. These guys will kill you! So, in my mind, this is as real as it gets, and we had to be on top of our game.

Pulling into Guy's house I felt good about the things we are about to get into. We happened to come across a .357 Magnum before leaving Houston but had no bullets. Guy must have talked about me like I was crazy. But trying to come up with ammo in Houston during this time was tough. Anyway, we went into his garage and by him being ex-military he had the ammo. In fact, he had .357 hollow point bullets and he loaded me up, and we were ready to roll. So, we headed out to this female's house I knew, she had become a good friend during my short stay. On our way over there, I just drove the guys around Killeen showing them all the spots that I knew about and some of the good people I knew. We were just having a good time meeting all kinds of women who were down for whatever.

It was getting late, so we started to head to her apartment. When we got over there, I just walked right in. She had food, drinks, and a few females over. So,the guys and I just chilled. She came out and informed us that they were about to go out for a few hours. She asked me was I going to still be here when she got back? I let her know that I would and that she needed to hurry back.

I can remember waking up to a gentle whisper, "Sam, Sam get up!" She was standing over me looking like an Angel, she was beautiful! I got up and we talked for what felt like a few minutes but wound up being most of the night. We finally fell asleep I guess around 3 a.m. in the morning. I woke up to my friends wanting something to eat. So, we got up and went searching for food. I spoke with Guy earlier to see when we were going to hook up. We agreed that we would hook up around 2 p.m. because he had some family things to get caught up on. So, we just hung around and waited on Guy to come over. So, we just got waisted and chilled with the females.

It's now December 21, 1992, a day I won't ever forget. The day started off like any normal day it was nice, sunny and crisp out and everybody was having a good time. My good friend, slash play brother Guy was on his way over and we were going to put the finishing touches on our new drug business plan. The routes we would take and the final cost of our whole selling.

Guy finally pulled up and came up the stairs. We kicked it for a while just getting caught up on everything that had been going on while I was back in Houston. In the meanwhile, I was unloading the gun and putting it on top of the entertainment system. We were so excited about what was about to kick off, our lives were about to go to a whole new level. Lots of money, lots of respect and for me a lot of women. Guy and I were so excited, Guy and Pat would be able to take better care of their families and for me, my mom wouldn't have to work ever again.

Guy and I were so excited that we began to play around just feeling good and having fun. So, in the midst of our playing around I reached up and grabbed the gun and aimed it at Guy. He opened his jacket and said, "Do what you have to do, homie!" We both knew that the gun was unloaded because he saw me unload it and put the bullets beside it. At least that was what we thought! I aimed the gun at him and pulled the hammer back. When I pulled the trigger, I heard nothing! All I remember is seeing a flash, and smoke. I looked over at Guy and we were looking eye to eye and suddenly, he just fell forward.

Now Guy was a prankster so I thought he was playing so I went over to him and told him to stop playing and to get up. What I saw next, would be burned into my mind forever. His eyes started rolling back into his head and his tongue started to jump and blood started flowing out of his mouth. I leaned over to look at the back of his head and there was a huge hole in the back of his head. I yelled for someone to call 911! But it was like everyone was in shock as to what just happened. All I knew was that my best friend was lying there on the ground with a bullet hole in his head. So, I basically jumped from the second floor of the apartments to the ground, I mean I hit about 1 or 2 steps and jumped the rest. All the while I'm in panic mode and thinking to myself, "This can't be happening!"

When I finally got to the pay phone, I called 911 and told them that my friend has been shot and we need help. From the time, I hung up, until the time the paramedics arrived until this very day is a blank. All I know is when the paramedics arrived they took Guy to the ambulance and all they told me was that they had a slight pulse and that they needed to get him to the hospital as soon as possible. At the same time, the Killeen police arrived and they began questioning us as to what had just happened. When they got to me, out of fear I told them that it was a drive-by shooting. But the officer kept asking me was I sure that that was what happened! I finally told him, no and that it was my fault because I was playing with a gun that I thought it was empty, but it went off. As they were taking me to the squad car, every fiber of my being was like, "this can't be happening!"

Until this day I cannot for the life of me remember the ride to the police department! All I remember is getting there and the detective asking me more questions and then placing me in a cell for the night. The next morning, I was escorted to the county jail and again placed in another holding cell. Only this time I was waiting to be processed into the county jail where I would have to wait until court. I was lying down in the holding cell and all of a sudden, this officer came to the glass knocking and pointing at me. I looked over at him like, "WHAT!" He motioned for me to come out and he asked me to take a look at the TV. Then he asked me, "is that you?" I had to take a double look because it was me! I was watching myself getting into a patrol car. But the only thing was that I didn't remember seeing and news people. It was all like I was in a bad dream and I couldn't wake up. I remember standing at the desk for what seemed like hours.

It was finally time! I was being assigned to my housing cell block. As the officers and I were heading to the elevator to go upstairs, I still couldn't seem to snap out of the daze I was in. As I entered the cell it was as though

I was a zombie, I mean I was numb. I just found a bunk and climbed in. I laid there and just tried to gather myself. I was like, this isn't for real I must be dreaming! This was crazy!

As the month's passed things began to change within me. For some reason, I wasn't experiencing any remorse and that was really bothering me. Guy was a good friend of mine, in fact, I loved him like a brother. I kept asking myself, "Why wasn't I feeling any remorse? This must not be real!" It was at this time that I began expecting a visit from him. Not in a spiritual way but in a natural way, like through the jail visitation system.

But there were other things that were going on, any type of loud noises would set me off. I became a nervous wreck and my emotions were all over the place. There actually came a time that I contemplated suicide. I told one of the guards that I was losing all hope and that I couldn't see myself living anymore. So, the guard took me out of the cell and put me in isolation. In other words, a padded room with a toilet in the floor. This time of my life was the hardest that I'd ever faced. I felt like I was losing my mind and nothing seemed to make sense.

As time went on, my court appointed lawyer was coming to see me from time to time. He was telling me that the State prosecutor was trying to charge me with murder and that they wanted the maximum. Now let me say this, for a court-appointed lawyer this guy worked like I was paying him. I told him that I was being totally honest with him. I informed him that there was no way that this could have been murder, both Guy and I thought that the gun was empty. So he suggested that we ask for a Lie Detector Test (LDT)and even though the test wasn't necessary it would be good for my case. After I passed the LDT the State dropped my case down to Involuntary Manslaughter, in which I could have received probation or prison time. Again, God was moving on my behalf and I didn't even have a clue.

As the months passed by I began to adapt to the county jail life from hustling food trays to getting tattoos. I had begun to drift into a darkness that I would later have a hard time getting out of. There would be Christian county jail ministries coming in and I would have fun just messing with them. At the time the only thing I could reflect back on was some of the Church of Christ teachings that I was raised on. I would argue that the only way to be saved was through water baptism. It even got to the point that some of the volunteers who would come in would come looking for me just to talk. After a while, I'd become a tank boss (i.e. a person who had seniority in the cell and status with the officers) and all the new arrivals would come to me for advice on what to expect in there. I just told them to stay to yourself and every-thing would be okay.

Then, right out of the blue, my lawyer came to see me and told me that he had some good news. So, being me, I was like, well, what is it? He told me that I was making bail, but that I would have to stay in Oklahoma until my court date; my grandparents on my father's side had posted bail for me. He said it would be in a couple of days, but it was about to happen. I think I had been in the county then for about eigh-teen months. After that meeting, I was ready for my ATW (i.e., All The Way), meaning I was about to be released out on bond. It was the early morning of the third day and I finally heard, "Samuel Jackson! ATW!" The guys in the cell rushed me so fast it wasn't funny; they wanted everything that I had. You see in jail whenever someone leaves, it's a custom to leave your stuff to some of the other inmates. After all the good-byes, I was headed out and that was a feeling like no other; but the burden of not knowing what was truly going to happen to me, in the long run, was painful.

I truly thought being on bond would make things a lot better, but it didn't! As a matter of fact, I believe it got worse. During this lying-in-wait phase of my life, the nightmares started; and these were some of the weirdest nightmares you could imagine. I can remember one in particular; it had to be one of the craziest dreams ever. I was running in this huge field of high grass and all of a sudden, this extremely large cobra head pops up out of the grass and starts to chase me. I can remember screaming because the cobra was right up on me; and right as he was about to take a plug out of me, I woke up screaming and in a cold sweat. I had plenty of dreams like these, and they would come on a regular basis for many years to come.

During my time out on bond was crazy. I stayed with my grandparents because they were the ones who bonded me out. Now staying with them meant you were going to be in church every time the doors were open, there were no if, and's or but's about it. I still wasn't seeking after God, and I still wasn't paying attention to the life lessons that they were trying to teach me. So, as time went on, I still didn't get it. I mean I was given every opportunity to get it right, but I just kept missing it. Anyway, I wound up staying in Lawton, Oklahoma just before I had to go back to court. This was a very memorable time; this was the time of my oldest son's conception. As I think back, I was so far away from God that it wasn't even funny; I was still just living life for the moment at hand.

Living life on bond was something else. Even though I was living a little on the crazy side. The thought of Guy never left my mind, I still couldn't believe it. But the constant reminder from my lawyer of my court date made it as real as could be. Time was drawing closer and closer for me to appear in court. And my nerves were a huge mess.

Then the call came. It was my lawyer and a court date had been set. I had a little over a week to get myself together and to get things in order. As the days passed I began to have feelings that things weren't going to end well. Now, to what extent! I didn't know.

The day had finally come, it was time to go back to Texas. The whole way down was like a blur it all seemed so foggy. I don't think I said two words the whole trip. As we continued to travel and get closer to Killeen, my nerves got really bad. Everything was about to get real and my life would never be the same again. My best friend was gone and it was all my fault.

Chapter 4

DOING TIME

As I'm standing before the judge, it's like my mind had left the building and I heard nothing for about ten to fifteen minutes. Then all of a sudden I hear the Judge yelling at me, "Mr. Jackson! Mr. Jackson!" "Yes, sir!" I respond. I just couldn't believe what was happening to me. The judge then asked me, "is there anything that I would like to say?" I turned to Guy's family and told them, that I was so sorry for what happened and that it was an accident. Guy's mother then told me that she forgave me and that she would pray for me. With tears in my eyes, I turned back to the judge and told him that was all. He then pronounced the ruling of my case: "Guilty of Involuntary Manslaughter!" And my sentence was 5 years TDCJ (i.e. Texas Department of Criminal Justice). I can remember it like it was yesterday, it felt like all the wind was knocked out of me. As the officers took me back to the holding cell, I just looked back at my grandfather and minister at the time and told them I was sorry. And that was the last I saw of them for a long time.

As I was going back to the county, I believe I was getting myself ready for what I was about to face. By this time, I had built a little reputation for myself. So, some of the officers knew me and the inmates did too. So, I pretty much did what I wanted to do. They let me become a trustee (i.e. an inmate who gets special privileges because they are following the rules) and that gave me some free reign over the jail. All the while I was getting myself mentally ready for what I was about to face. All I knew was that I had 5 years, so I was thinking 5 years of my life belonged to the state of Texas.

During this time in my life, I kind of kept my mom at a distance. I didn't want her to see me like this. I got myself into all of this so I had to deal with it. I didn't call and I didn't write for a while.

I would spread my hustle while I was in the county jail. I would transport contraband from cell to cell. And that's how I would get my extra snacks, stamps, and hygiene. I had to survive like this for a few months.

It was getting closer and closer to the time for me to leave for TDCJ. And my nerves were all over the place. I had no clue what I was about to face. And to be honest I was scared out of my mind.

The time finally arrived and all my fears would finally become a reality. I was on the chain and I would be at my assigned Unit in a matter of hours. I was headed to the Gurney Unit in Palestine, Texas which was way out of the way for my mom to come see me. So, this meant I would be doing my time by myself. No visits! And the calls were collect and long distance. So, that was out! All this was going through my mind on the way there, and it was tearing my heart to pieces.

We finally made it to the Unit and it was crazy. The officers were all yelling and talking bad to you, and you couldn't do anything about it, you just had to take it. When I finally got to the cage, I was packed in with the rest of the guys like a bunch of dogs, then they begin calling us out for processing. The processing phase is so humiliating, they shaved my head and made me shave off all my facial hair. They tried to strip me of all my dignity and to an extent they did. My name wasn't Samuel D Jackson Jr anymore, it was #671205. I was now no longer a person with a name but a number for the state. Yes, like cattle! And then you're herded off to classification to get your housing assignment.

It seemed as though this process would never end. However, it did, but what came next was far worse. The assignment of our work details and how the process took place. You had to go through a medical evaluation, and that was kind of funny in a way. You had to take a gang of shots and that was something to witness. You had hardened criminals crying like babies, I mean with the whimpering and heavy breathing it was a sight to see. Murders, thieves and rapist balling like babies, the worst of our society. Never would have seen that coming in a million years.

After all the shots and the physicals, you were handed a piece of paper if it had "1AGG", it meant, "1 aggie please". And that meant you would be on the chain gang, like in the movies. This was now my life and I had to get used to it. I was in a cell block with a bunch of youngsters and even though I was a youngster myself I was still older than a bunch of the guys. Some of them were 16 and 17 years old, they had just been certified as adults. And they were wild and crazy! They would get a kick out of making the guards mad for no reason at all. They would get the whole block racked up (i.e. everyone sent to their bunks). It was crazy!

I can remember the first day I went into the fields. It was at least over 100 degrees that day and the field officers acted like they had a bet going, on seeing whose squad could go the longest and the hardest. This was some hard work and the places we had to work, oh my God! Now I'm from 5th ward and some of the things we had to do I had no clue.

It was this one day that we were working in what they called a maize field. It consisted of corn stalks, maize stalks and something called Johnson grass. The field officer who was assigned to us told me to cut the Johnson grass and I was like, "Man I'm from 5th Ward! Does it look like I know what Johnson grass is?" He just started laughing and said, "it's the tall blades of grass between the maize and the corn stalks. Just hit it at the root and let it lay!" So, I did. As I was going down my side I ran up on this huge spider and I mean huge, it looked like a little fist with legs. So, I did what any normal guy would do, I jumped into the other lane and went around it. Then got back in my lane when I passed it.

I hate to say it, but some of those experiences were something else. And I do mean something else. There were times when our squad was just crazy, I think the average age was about 19 years old and we were out of control. We would grab some of our homeboys from other cell blocks and just wrestle with them in our cell blocks. It was insane!

But as time went on, I began to reflect back on what I truly needed in

my life. I began to go to the church services that were being held. And I have
to say I believe the Lord was beginning to move in my life. I was getting
involved in some of the volunteer work
that the offenders could do. I was on the
chair set-up crew for a long time and I
was happy like I'd never been before. I
would study my bible in the cell block
and even study with other offenders. It
was like I was a new person.

I was seeing things in a whole new
light, my view on life was beginning to
change. I was becoming more social
with other offenders and I was beginning to witness to other offenders and
there was no fear. I began inviting guys
to our services and it was going pretty
good. Until I came across this one

guy and he challenged me to attend one of his services. So, I said, "okay no problem! What service is that?" I thought it may have been one of the other Christian services. So, I said, "so what service do you want me to attend?" He said, "Islamic services!" I agreed and it would change me for life.

I would go to the Islamic services every Saturday, just to hear the guest speakers. And they wouldn't hold anything back. They were mad at our government and the way they spoke, it sounded dead on. They were studious and well learned, and that was foreign to me. School and learning was just not for me. But they encouraged studying because knowledge was power. So, I started studying different things and I was actually retaining some knowledge. It was freaking me out!

I'd gone to the Saturday meetings which are called Talim services for about a year and a half. I began to walk with more confidence and wouldn't hesitate to speak out on certain things that I thought weren't right. I quit playing as much and got very serious about almost everything. I was becoming a new person and I mean a brand-new person, my old way of thinking was slowly beginning to fade away. I was studying to improve on myself and thinking for myself for once in my life.

As time moved on I found myself with a decision that I had to make. Would I embrace Islam or stay with the religion that I was raised up in? I was stuck, but I knew that I had to decide. I went to one last church service just to see if God had a word for me. When I didn't perceive one I knew what I had to do. So around June or July of 1994, I accepted Islam and became a Muslim.

I felt like a new person, my understanding on life was new and I had a new-found knowledge of a lot of different things. I was no longer the reckless youth who acted off impulse, but a thinking man. My understanding was at a new level and my insight was crazy. I believed that I finally found the truth and that I was serving a purpose greater than myself. Islam had my full attention and I was on cloud nine.

Embracing Islam kind of made my time a little easier, as funny as that may sound. I was learning how to fight the system in the way that it should be fought and I was fighting it pretty well. Instead of getting all crazy with the youngsters, I would play chess with the older offenders. Chess seemed to calm me down and it allowed me to focus more. It's what we called a thinking man's game. Before chess the only thing that I was good at was spades. But chess was on a whole new level. It was fun, to try and out think the other player. It showed me how to look at life, especially life in prison and that was a tool that I definitely needed. Chess taught me how to look a few moves ahead in life. Basically, it taught me how to pay attention to details.

During this time in my life I was becoming a new person and I liked who I was becoming. I was growing up; I was becoming a man. As time went on, I was getting deeper and deeper into Islam and I was moving up. I finally realized that I had the capacity to learn and it was exciting. I was learning how to deal with the officers and the offenders on a totally different level. Things didn't get to me as much as it did in the past. I was learning how to face my problems and deal with them in a manly way. Something that I never did in the past, I just pushed them to the side or handled them in foolish ways. It was more on the foolish side most of the times, though.

Doing time was an experience that I never thought I could do, it was a world of its own. The things you had to go through were something else. Prison would either make you stronger or break you in half. But I had decided that nothing was going to break me, NOTHING! I don't know if it was because I had become a Muslim or that it was already in me. But whatever it was, I knew that I wasn't going to let the prison life get to me. I had to do better for myself, I was not going to waste my time on playing games and letting my time just pass me by. I once had an old man tell me, "What's the most important asset in life that once it's gone you can never get it back?" I told him I didn't know. He said, "TIME!" And that stuck with me. I began to understand that every moment was precious and that I needed to be building on each moment and not waste my time on silly things.

Prison life, regardless of how you slice it, is never a good thing. But how you do your time makes all the difference. From December 1992 to February of 1995 which was 2 years and 3 months, I went from the Bell County jail to the Gurney Unit to the Larry Gist Unit. I went from a high school drop out to a GED recipient and I went from Christian to Muslim. I was a different person and kind of liked the new guy, to be honest with you. I was finally finishing things that I had started. I was no longer the person that left things undone, I was no longer the person who lived life by the seat of his pants. I had vision and ambition to finally be something in life and nothing was going to stop me.

The time came, and I was finally up for parole. I must have waited for about a month for my answer and when the answer finally came it was good news. I had received an FI-1 which meant I had made parole and would be going home within the month. I was finally about to get out and see my family again. Especially my grandmother and grand-father. I had been telling my grand-mother to just hold on until I get out so I could see her just one more time. You see she was suffering from chronic heart failure. But she was strong and determined to see me get out. And on

February 5, 1995, I was released from the Larry Gist Unit and headed home to Houston. Life was good again and I was a new man on top of all that. When I got to the bus station in Houston, TX. I went outside and tried to get a cab. But when I told them where I was trying to go most of them told me that they didn't go to 5th Ward anymore. However, I finally got a cab and he took me home. When I got to my grandparents' house I knocked on the door and my middle brother answered the door with this deep voice. "Who is it?" I told him it's me man open the door. He said, "me who?!" So, I told him, "it's Sam fool! Open up!" So, he finally did and the reunion began.

Chapter 5

MISTAKEN IDENTITY

L ife in the free world is a lot different when you have some sense or shall I say when you finally know how to think. However, prison taught me a lot about seeing people for who they really are and for what they really want. I was on a path and it was a good one, I knew what I wanted and knew what steps I needed to take in order to get there. After I had been home for a few weeks, I began looking for work but ran into problem after problem. However, I tried to stay focused by attending Islamic services and staying on top of my religious duties.

I tried staying with my mom for a while, but really there was no room at her place. Luckily, my younger brother right under me had an apartment and I could stay with him and his girl until I was able to get on my feet. Now before I got incarcerated, I not of sound and sober mind. But during my incarceration, my brother had gotten involved in the street life. He had all the connections and I mean he knew everybody.

Before I left, my brother was about his education, he was heading somewhere and I feel like I messed all that up. I feel as though I lead him down a deep dark path to nowhere, a path that took all his dreams and aspirations away, and that was on me. But like always I thought about that for a while and then I pushed it to the back of my mind in order to move forward. Soon I was back into the swing of things, and was back to indulging in my bad behaviors, but it was a little different this time. I wasn't running the streets and getting into trouble anymore, I was doing everything at home.

I think it was about a month later and everything that I had set out to do, just fell by the wayside. You see, I learned something about myself. By me relapsing, it killed my ambition to want to continue in bettering myself. All I wanted to do was get high and drunk. I slacked off on all my Islamic duties and being a Muslim was no longer important to me. I didn't have to act upright anymore because no one was watching me. In other words, there was no accountability held. So, I returned back to what I knew, and that was the street life. But again, it was on a different level this time. I was around my brothers and their friends, when I was indulging in my habits, it wasn't in the projects or the streets.

After a while, the smoking got real intense and we would dip our sweets (i.e. weed rolled in Swisher Sweets cigar leaves) in codeine or syrup, otherwise known as lean. I was burning up all my little brain cells! And the positive thinking that I was doing before I was released went up in smoke just like the weed. I would smoke weed almost every day, the only time I would stop would be when it was getting close for me to see my parole officer. And that was the only time that I would stop. I was drinking again and even eating pork from time to time. I had slipped back into the old me again.

Now the thing about getting back into drugs, other criminal activities tend to follow. Before I knew it, I was getting back into the street life. Doing a little hustling here and there just to keep my habits going was starting to take place on a regular basis. The standards that I set for myself were quickly dropping to an all-time low. This was not who

I had envisioned myself to be. But for reasons beyond me I just couldn't stop!

I had so many plans for myself! The goals that I'd set for myself prior to my release from prison were well thought out and planned to the tee. Some of it stemmed from drugs, but the different relationships I had developed over the time played a big part in it too. I was so eager to be with a woman that I didn't take the time out to really get to know them. It was all about the wrong things. It was all about what a woman could do for me and I guess that stemmed from my earlier years of witnessing so many unhealthy relationships and the molestation that I went through. All I knew was that it was all about me. PERIOD!

I can remember a time, I was dating this one female and seeing another. But the one I was dating knew about the other woman, because I told her that the other woman was giving me money and buying me all sorts of things. So, I told my girl that I would get the money from the other woman and spend it on her. And she was okay with it, which I really didn't care if she would be or not at the time.

The other woman would get me anything that I wanted. I would just tell my girl that I was going to be at her place for a few days and when I got back we would go shopping and have a good time. But I never did any of those things. Lying came so easy to me, I guess because I really didn't care if she believed me or not. I felt like I would just try anything, just to see if I could get away with it. And most of the time I did!

But like most things that were going on in my life at this time, the other woman didn't last long. I decided that I would try being a one-woman man for a change. But I was still going to do my own thing, I didn't want to answer to anyone. I was becoming numb to how other people felt, it was about me and how I felt. I was arrogant and cocky, no one could tell me anything. Nothing!

I was feeling myself and getting bolder by the second. I was forgetting who or what I wanted to be. It was beginning to be all about this certain image I thought I had to uphold. An image that my hood glorified, being an ex-con. You see, in my hood being an ex-con was a rite of passage, if you hadn't been to prison you weren't a man. Every grown man that I knew in my hood had been to prison. And they had the utmost respect, from everyone! They were repeat offenders, meaning they were in and out of the prison system. Some you could say, grew up in prison because they went in at a young age and by the time you saw them again they were old men. But that's just the way it was and some of us as young men thought that was kool, self-included.

It was a sick way of looking at life, but that's what it was. And as sad as it may sound some of the youngsters in my hood including myself couldn't see themselves making it to 21. In fact, we couldn't see ourselves making it to the next month, it was about the now and then. And I was headed right back to that line of thinking and that was scary. It was like I was getting drawn right back into that life.

Speaking of my hood and the rite of passage we sought, I can remember when I was released from prison and my brother and I went down to the Kelly Courts. We decided to check on some old friends and those same old friends were sitting in what seemed like the same spots, doing and talking about the same stuff. It was like nothing had changed, no growth! Nothing! In fact, a few of them walk up to me with a weird sense of excitement, so weird that what they said next, I just couldn't grasp. One of them came to me and asked, "Man what's it like down there? I'm about to go down there real soon!" With this huge smile on his face! He was looking forward to going to prison. So, I told him, "it's no fun down there, trust me!" However, the idea of his excitement really bothered me, more so, it was disturbing. These things would cross my mind on a regular basis.

I believe it was going on about my sixth month of being out and I was finally starting to get a grip. I started back going over to my grandparents' house on a more regular basis. I would sit and talk with them about everything, and other times I would just sit and listen to their wisdom. I actually felt as though I was getting it together.

Things were beginning to look up for me. FINALLY, things were turning around!

I continued to visit my grandparents on a frequent basis, just trying to spend as much time with them as I could. I would tell them about the dreams and the aspirations that I had and how frustrated I was about getting off track. I wanted to make them so proud of me! I just felt like I owed them that. Mainly because of all that they'd done for me, and our family.

They would listen to me rant and rave, but they would always give me some encouraging words to think about, especially my grandfather. Just to show you how funny my grandfather was. I can remember a time when I was talking to him and he wasn't looking directly at me. So, I said, "Pawpaw you're not looking at me!" He kindly continued to pour his coffee and said, "boy I hear with my ears, not with my eyes, now say what you have to say!" So, I went on to tell him about the things that were on my mind at the time. My grandpa would just blow me away with the way he would say things.

After a while, I was beginning to really get things together. But little did I know that all was about to change. On August 19, 1995, my world was about to get turned upside down. But let me back up to the 18th. I just so happened to stop by my grandparents' house to check on them and have a little chat, and my uncle Donald was over there. I thanked my grandmother for sticking around until I got out of prison because I knew she was sick and she had already had a few strokes in the past and had to get a pacemaker. And it was just a matter of time. I think we talked for hours just reminiscing over the past. We had a good time! But it was getting late and me and my uncle both had to get home.

Little did I know that this would be the last time that I would see my granny alive. The following morning, I was awakened by a phone call from my aunt Carolyn who was very disturbed at the time. I'll never forget her words, "Peewee you need to get over here right now! It's your granny!" I knew right then she had passed away and it knocked the wind out of me. I ran the whole way to her house and that must have been at least 2 to 3 miles. I can't even remember if I stopped by my brothers' apartment or not to tell him. But anyway, when I finally arrived, everyone was standing in the den starring and very quiet. As I walked into the living room I saw my granny lying on her daybed face down, dead. It appeared like she was trying to take off her stockings throughout the night and just passed away. As I was looking for my grandfather, I heard this loud cry from the kitchen. It was my grandfather screaming out my granny's name, "Ola! Ola! Ola! Don't leave me! Please, don't leave me!" I just ran to him and just held him. This day changed everything for me. I know because for the next few weeks I simply have no memory, every-thing is just a blank. Everything!

After the passing, away of my grand-mother, I just lost myself. I believe I was suffering from mistaken identity due to grief. I was like a zombie, just stumbling my way through, lost. I was trying to work as a maintenance man for the apartments that I was staying in. Because at this time, I had my lady and we were expecting a baby. So, I was trying to make a way for them, but the money wasn't coming quick enough. Those so call friends had started coming around and offering all the wrong kind of help. However, I was getting des-perate so I took a little help here and there. And that still wasn't enough. I had lost all sense of who I was! I believe

I went a whole month just drifting about not knowing who or what I was. September of 1995 was kind of a blank. I only remember the end of September, because one of the apartments in our little complex caught fire and the landlord asked me how long would it take to get it up to speed. The guy before me had started on it, but he was a crack head and he was dragging it out. I was doing other things at the time. So, she asked me to get on top of it and try to get it done within 90 days. So, I started on it and I would be up for like 48 hours straight. It was free rent, so it was something that I had to do. And I was doing it.

However, I still had my pregnant woman at the apartment and things weren't getting any easier. Then along comes this friend of mine and he has this hustle that we can make some serious money from. So, he tells me about this liquor store that's a front for drugs, and that we can go and case it out to see when would be a good time for us to rob the place. I was a little reluctant at first because the offer just came out of nowhere. But I eventually gave in and we cased the place for about 3 days. In between those times, I was working like a crazy man all day and all night trying to make ends meet. Plus, my woman was having cravings out of this world, it was crazy. But I was trying to get it!

It was October 5, 1995, a day that I will never forget. My homeboy came by earlier during the day and we decided that this was the day. So, he ran down the plan to me as to how we were going to do it. I was a little foggy minded at the time because I had pulled an all-nighter the night before and I was spent mentally, not to mention physically. But it was set and there was no backing out of it now. Even though I truly believe God had given me a way out that night, I was too stupid to recognize it. My child's mother begged me not to go and even her mother came over and tried to stop me. But I wasn't having it, I was determined to go and get that money. She even asked me to go and get her some donuts and I did. But I dropped them off and we rolled out to go and hit our little ole *lick* (i.e. hustle, grind or commit a crime).

On our way, my boy handed me a little .25 automatic handgun, but for some reason it was empty. For some reason, I didn't question it, I guess because I was so tired and I just left it alone. We talked a little more about our plan and how we expected it to go and it seemed flawless. The security guard was supposed to leave and be gone for about 15 minutes and it should be an in and out job. As we made it to the parking lot we sat out there waiting until the guard left. My nerves at this time, were on edge and I was getting scared. So, my so-called friend told me to just calm down and everything would work out as planned because there was no backing out now. This was the only time that we had to do this. So, I gathered myself together by taking deep breaths and pumping myself up to do the job. I was ready!

I jumped out of the car as soon as I saw the guard leave and made my way to the store. As I approached the door I saw just a woman on the inside and she was behind the counter and there was no one else inside. So, I went in and made like I was looking for something to drink but couldn't find it. So, she asked me what I was looking for and I told her that I was looking for I nice wine to celebrate a friend's promotion. So, she came out from behind the counter and came over to me and began to show me a few wines that she thought would be nice. As soon as she turned her back to me, I grab her from behind and placed the gun in the small of her back and told her to take me to the stash where they kept their drug money. Then she did something that totally caught me off balance. She reached backward and tried to grab the gun from my hand and I just freaked out. I began moving her towards the cash register and telling her to give me all the cash that they had. At this time, the guard was coming through the doorway, way too early! He saw me and reached for his gun and told me to let the woman go and to give myself up. Now, I began to think real hard as to what I was going to do next.

A lot of things flashed through my mind at this time. This was also around the time that O.J. Simpson beat his case and the police officers were going crazy. I thought about my unborn child and if I tried to fight my way out, I could be killed. So, I raised the gun in the air and told the guard that I surrender and I laid down on the floor. My mind was racing a million mile a minute! How could this have happened? HPD finally came and they just put me in the back of the patrol car, not saying a word. It was a little scary, let me stop, I was scared out of my mind. At this time, HPD was known to be a bit dangerous and I didn't know what was about to happen.

Once I was put into the car, a few officers would walk by and tell me they wished I would have tried to run, because it would have given them some target practice. It seemed like we were there forever, I just wanted to get to the station and get things started. After about what seemed like hours the officers finally pulled off and we were headed to the station. It was the most horrific ride of my life! Once again, I was in over my head, only this time it was no accident.

As we pulled up to the station all I could do was sigh and take a deep breath, because I knew I'd messed up. I was on parole and I had committed a new crime, with a handgun, I knew I was going back to prison. Because for one, what I'd done warranted a parole volition. Two, it was a crime with a handgun with intent to commit bodily harm. I knew I was in big trouble and that I was headed back to the life that I swore I would never return to.

As my mind began to clear a little, I realized that I was in the county jail in the holding cell, and I had this feeling like I had never been out of prison and that the time I spent on the streets was just a dream. The holding cell was the worst 2 hours of my life! Having to be packed in with a bunch of drunks and people from off the streets made the smell unbearable. I was just ready to get to my cell and make some calls and then go to sleep. People were stepping all over each other and everyone was just waiting to be called out to be processed.

Finally, my name was called and they took me through the whole process: the fingerprinting, the mug shot, the shower for bugs, the medical interview and finally the dress out. After all that, I waited for another 15 to 20 minutes and then I was finally classified to my cell block where people of like crimes are housed. As I made it to my cell block and stepped into the cell it was like I had never been released and the eight months in the free world, was nothing but a dream. Sitting on my bunk all I could think about was how I had my life planned out and how I saw myself living before I was released from prison the first time. And now because I was suffering from mistaken identity, I was back in the same situation I was in eight months ago.

Chapter 6

A DECADE AND A HALF

It must have been almost a week, and finally, I was going to court to see who my court appointed lawyer would be. As I was waiting in the holding cell, this man walked up to the cell door and asked for a Samuel Jackson. I immediately spoke up and made my way to the door. He then held out his legal pad and told me this is what the DA is offering you. I was like, "what!" he said, "it's on the paper". I looked all over that page and all I saw was scribble and off to the left, I saw what I thought was 40 agg. (i.e. *aggravated*). So, I look up at him and said, "all I see is scribble and what looks like 40 agg., and that can't be what they're talking about". He looked at me and said, "Mr. Jackson that's exactly what they're offering." And on top of the 40 agg., the charge was Aggravated Robbery.

I couldn't believe it! For one, the gun wasn't loaded and no money was taken. If anything the charges should have been Attempted Robbery with intent to commit bodily harm. But when you're ignorant of the law and you have a court appointed lawyer the State can get away with just about anything. So, after our meeting was over, and I didn't

take the plea by the way! I began vis-
iting the Law Library on a regular basis.
Hoping to find something that would
help my case.

Now the Law Library in any
Correctional Facility has what are
known as jailhouse lawyers. And these
guys can get out almost anyone, except
themselves. But they will research your
case as if their very own lives depended
on it. So, I began checking out a few of
the inmates who were pretty good and
after that, I had to narrow it down to
the best one. Because you don't want
your business all over the jail. Anyway, I
finally found one and he went at it hard.
The first question he asked me was did
they read you your rights? Which the
answer was "NO!" And he said, "okay

let's stop right there!" He then told me, that, that in itself should get my case thrown out. After hearing that I asked to return to my cell so that I could call my lawyer and share with him my findings. I think I must have called him all day, but to no avail. And when I finally did get a hold of him which was about two weeks later. He wasn't trying to hear anything I had to say. The only thing he was trying to do was get me to sign for some time, it was very tiring and frustrating.

After realizing that my lawyer wasn't out for my benefit, but for the states. I had to find out what I could do to change that. So I ask the jailhouse lawyer what could I do to fix my situation. He mentioned to me that I could file a writ to fire my lawyer. So I filed the writ and it was shot down by the Judge. So I was stuck with a lawyer who wouldn't fight for me. I don't know what the problem was with my lawyer but I wouldn't see him for months at a time.

Now, in the meantime, I was stuck in the county and that was no picnic. It was cold all the time and the guards were mean as all get out. I never had any problems with the inmates, because it was basically all homeboys. As a matter of fact, one of the inmates and I had one thing in common. The guy I went to commit the crime with, well we both knew him in a unique way. He had set him up just like I came to find out he did me. Little did I know, he was known for setting up different guys all over

Houston. When I found that out, I was furious, and for a long time I wanted to kill that guy. I was in a bad way, mentally and spiritually I was truly lost.

As time went by my lawyer was beginning to show me that he was trying to help me out. He informed me that I was getting a new DA and that we might have some luck with him. I think it was after the holidays that my lawyer came to see me and told me that we may be able to get a reduction on my time. But he didn't want to make me any promises. So he said he would get back to me in about a week or so.

After about a week I was getting called out to go to court and boy was I nervous. I didn't know what was about to happen all I knew was that my lawyer told me that we might get some favor from this new DA. When I finally arrived at court my nerves were all over the place I could barely keep still. And out of know where my lawyer pops up and tells me that we have been rescheduled, and that was a good thing. I think it was around November and he said that we should try and push everything back until after the holidays, because timing is everything. Man, was I relieved! I didn't know what was about to happen.

I was so messed up with what was happening, that I began to really question what it was that I believed in. I never heard of any Islamic services that were going on, so I started reading the bible that I came across. During this time of my life, I didn't know if I was muslim or christian. It seems that I was trying to use God to get me out of the mess I was in. So I tried everything, I began talking, walking and acting like a Christian. I even did a little meditating from time to time. I was trying to get myself out of this mess.

As the months went by I was praying for the impossible, I was hoping that my case would be thrown out. But I wouldn't be so lucky. It was about a week after New Years and I was called out for court. I was feeling good for some reason and I was eager to see what was about to happen. As I sat in the holding cell with the other inmates awaiting our fates, I suddenly became very calm. About 15 minutes later, my lawyer shows up and he is smiling, I automatically jump up and run to the bars. "So what's the news?" He looked at me with a slight grin and told me that the DA wanted to give me a gift. I was like so what's the gift?! He told me that the offer was now 18 years and that was a belated Christmas gift. So, I thought for a while and finally told him that I would take it. So now it was official, my second journey to prison was underway.

As I returned to the cell block I quickly began to make phone calls to my family letting them know what had just happened. My family was upset about my decision because they truly didn't understand what my time meant. They thought I had to do the whole 18 years. It was a bittersweet moment, but I was finally moving on. I finally got a hold of my girlfriend and told her what had just happened and she went crazy. So, that weekend she came up to the jail to see me. She went to talking about getting married and how she was going to be by my side the whole time. I told her that I was going to be away for 9 years for sure, because on an 18-aggravated year sentence in 1995, you would have to do 9 years before you would be eligible for parole. So, I knew it would be a while this time, and I told her that she wouldn't make it.

She cried and pleaded that she would stay with me, but I knew she would get tired and move on. In fact, I told her, that she would come to see me every weekend while I was in the county jail and once I was moved to a prison farm the visits would slack off until they stopped completely. And then the letters would stop and then out of the blue the plea for a divorce would come. So, she cried and cried that that would not happen, but I knew that it would. This went on for about 30 minutes and I finally got tired and told her to do whatever she wanted. I didn't want to have to worry about a family while I was away. Because I saw how all that went, the first time I went down.

During my county jail stay, I made the most out of my time. I took up a few courses, I enrolled in a Graphic Arts class and then a Business class. I was trying to get a grip on my life even though I was facing some serious time. I looked for Islamic services but for some reason, nothing. So, I would read the bible and I even started going back to Christian services.

As time went on, it started to settle in, that I was going to be gone for a very long time. I asked my mom to come see me, because I needed to talk to her about something very serious. The weekend finally came and it was just me and mom out in visitation, no girlfriend and no brothers. So, we talked and I can remember telling her that there was no need for anyone else in our family to ever go to prison because I was doing enough time for everyone in our family. Nine years was a long time, and that was just to be eligible for a parole hearing.

As I was getting myself mentally prepared for prison, I got called out for court again. For some reason, I could not figure out why! When I finally made it to the holding cell an officer came and asked me if I had a change of clothes. Now, I was worked up, I thought I was getting released. So, I asked, "what's going on?" He looked surprised and asked me if I knew that I was getting married! I was like, "no sir!" So, he told me that that's why I was called out. So, I was like okay and I got married.

During the rest of my county time, time went by kind of quick and before I knew it, I was on the chain (i.e. being transported to prison) and heading for TDCJ. Like last time it was the same old process, in regards to getting processed in. Only this time I knew what to expect and how to maneuver. I wasn't a new boot anymore I was a 2-time offender. And I was somebody in the prison world, I had what you could call rank.

For some reason, I started going to the church services on the unit and was getting involved in some of the activities. I was doing good, I was learning a lot about Christianity but the Holy Spirit part I wasn't getting. So I kind of faked my way through it the whole time. By me being a repeat offender I was able to work my way out of the field squad. I managed to work my way into the Unit Supply Department and that job was great. I had the run of the whole unit and I even had a key to all the restrooms. In the prison world, I had status, I had made it.

During my stay on the Holiday Unit, I was blessed to finally meet my daughter Jasmine. She was the most beautiful baby I had ever seen. After our visit, I just took her scent back with me to my dorm and just wept. I thought about not being there for her and my son Trevon because of my stupid decision to try and go robbing. It was then that I decided that this life wasn't for me. I had to get my head on straight but I didn't know where to start. I just knew it had to be done.

I believe I stayed on the Holiday Unit for about fourteen months and I was doing well for myself. I remember going into work one morning and my supervisor told me that the Major of the Unit was promoted to Warden in west Texas and that one of us would be getting transferred to help open the new Unit. It was about 3 to 4 days later and I was told to pack all my things because I was on the chain. Leaving on the chain for a Unit is a bit different from the chain leaving the county jail. Reason being even though you're in prison you meet some good people, and you develop some true friendships. But you must go and try and finish out your time. So, it's a little bittersweet!

It took about two days to get to the new unit and we had to stop at a couple of the worst units in Texas. But to see the free world and go clear across Texas was worth it. Plus, I didn't have a choice in the matter. Being on the road again was nice, the only bad thing was you couldn't see out of the windows because of the metal screen that was bolted to every passenger window on the bus. It made you feel like a dog in the back of a truck.

When we finally arrived at the Dick Ware Unit it was like a ghost town, we were the first batch to arrive. And if I'm not mistaken, our first night, we had a red dirt storm that messed up everything in the dorms. We were cleaning up to what seemed like all night and the next morning and it was some serious work. Red dirt is no joke; it gets into everything and it stains everything. But we got it done.

As time moved on, I'd say about three months later. The unit was fully functional and running smoothly. The education department was off and running and that meant religious services were going. I took a few college classes and I was going to church. But something still wasn't right, I was still missing something. In our dorm, we started what we called "Think Tank Sessions". And believe me, we came up with some topics to toss around. Men tend to be good at that.

However, there was this Muslim guy there and he was very intelligent and that was sparking my interest. It made me think back to when I was truly practicing Islam. So again, I started going back to the services and seeking again. It wasn't long before I'd taken the Shahada (i.e. the pledge to be a Muslim) again, and once again I was a practicing Muslim. Only this time things would be a lot different.

As I got deeper and deeper into Islam this time, I began to consider my case again. Only this time I began to realize that my case had been enhanced and that meant my case started at 15 to life. That was due to my previous case because both had a deadly weapon attached to them. And that was why I couldn't get any amount of time under 10 years. Which meant I had to do 15 years flat before I could be released. And that was a hard pill to swallow.

I began to grow in knowledge and understanding in this junction of my life. And it felt good! I was doing better in school and in my religious studies. I was moving up the ranks of Islam at a very fast pace. As time went on, I'd forgotten that I only had about six months left on this unit because I'd done 14 months on the Holiday Unit. And time was getting close!

It was around the middle of November of 1998 and I was on the chain again. But this time it wasn't to a State Jail facility, it was to my first TDCJ–ID Unit, a real prison. And this time, I had to go through the Goree Unit in Huntsville, this is where they classify you according to your case. So, if you're a bad actor you go to a unit where there are bad actors, at least that's what was supposed to happen.

But sometimes people slipped through the cracks. But anyway, I was assigned to Briscoe Unit and this unit was near one of the borders of Mexico. It was way out there in the boonies.

Now Briscoe was a different world from what I was used to. This unit was filled to the hilt with gangs. It had the Bloods and the Crips, the Mexican Mafia, Tongo, Arian Brothers, Arian Circle, Black Gangster Disciples and the Muslims. And each one of these had groups that split from them. And it seemed that almost every thug I knew in Houston was there. This unit was crazy; everything went on there.

But I had it made, because as soon as you get to your dorm the offenders begin to drill you with question after question. And when they found out I was from 5th Ward I was in like flin, and on top of that, I was a Muslim. I found out very quickly that the Muslims and 5th Ward had a little power on this unit. Some of the guys would bring you a care package (i.e. toothpaste, stamps, envelopes, and coffee) just to hold you over until you could make commissary. Which was alright, but you had to be careful who you excepted those things from. Because some of the guys would make you think that they were sincere and the next thing you know the tables would get turned on you out of nowhere. You had to be alert always!

The Briscoe Unit was where I learned to do my time. In a way, you could say that I learned how to move around within the system and being able to do that, can make or break you while doing time. When I first arrived, I was assigned to the Hoe Squad but by then I had learned the lay-in game. Now the lay-in game was simple, all you had to do was submit two or three I-60's (i.e. Inter-office communication forms) every day and you would get a lay-in from work the next day. I managed to pull this off until I could get a job change from the hoe squad to the yard squad.

I have to admit, Briscoe was a little exciting, everything went on at that unit! I met some of the most interesting people there, some were real cut throat and some were just trying to be better people. It was then that I learned, that you must hang around the people that you want to be like. So, here I was again, at another crossroad in my life. Do I want to be a career criminal or do I want to make something out of myself? And I had to make this decision for me and for me only.

As I contemplated on what I wanted to do, I began to put in a request for another job change. I wanted to do something that would help me, for whenever I got released, something dealing with computers. But that didn't happen as soon as I'd liked it too. I received a job change alright, but it was to the Maintenance Department. Now that was okay, but I didn't have any skills for that job. But I did learn a few things that would help me out in the long run.

I can remember a time when we were turning out for work and I had a crook in my neck. And it was killing me! And a friend of mine told me that he could get it out quick. So, I took him up on it and it was the worst mistake I could've made. I walked around the unit for about a week with a huge knot in my neck. When I finally made it to medical, the PA told me that it was because I smoked weed. Now that was a lie because I hadn't smoked weed in about 4 years. But that's what you had to deal with in prison.

While in maintenance I was put on the building maintenance crew and that was fun. We would go around the whole unit fixing things and getting a chance to kick it with some of our friends. The officer we had with us was very nice, he didn't sweat us at all if we did our jobs. But again, I was getting restless and I wasn't satisfied. So, I put in to be a clerk and that was when I began to understand what I was good at. Being a clerk allowed me access to computers, even though there was no internet access, I learned a lot.

As time moved on, I gained skills that I never thought I had. I was making documents from scratch and building databases. And the respect that I gained from the officers blew my mind. But again, I was feeling like I needed more. I was moving up the ladder in the Islamic religion and that was great, but it still wasn't enough. I needed more and I wasn't getting it.

There were rumors going around about getting hardship moves. Meaning you could get moved closer to home if you had a sick loved one. All you had to do was get your loved one to contact their State Rep., and inform them of your medical condition, and why your love one couldn't make the trip to come see you. But our State Rep. wouldn't do it. So, I had to try and figure out another way to get closer to home.

In my efforts to get moved, I signed up to go to college and since Briscoe didn't have a college there, I knew I would have to be sent to another prison. And I was hoping that it would be near Houston. So, I began to send in request after request to go to college. Finally, after a long wait, the education department laid me in and had me fill out my paperwork. I was so excited; I didn't know what to do. Just the thought of getting closer to home was so exciting, this would mean that I could see my mom a little more often.

It must have been about a month later and I was getting called out for the chain. I was on my way, happy as can be. So, we make it to our first stop which was about 30 minutes down the road and the guard makes the announcement that "if I call your name start making your way to the front of the bus to get off." When he gets to the "J's", my name is the first name he calls. It was like I had the wind knocked out of me. I got moved alright, but it was nowhere near Houston, in fact, it was just down the highway to the Torres Unit.

The feeling I had when I arrived at Torres was kind of strange, it was a feeling that I'd never experienced before. I had a boldness about myself that I'd never had before. The experiences of being on those units taught me a lot about myself. Don't get me wrong, there is a level of fear that comes over you but it's more of a fear of the unknown. But once you realize that this is happening and that there's nothing you can do about it; you just relax and get ready for what's next.

So, the first day on Torres was good! I think I had lay-ins all day, one to medical, classification and the last one was to the education department. And when I said all day that's just what it was, all day. Medical was for my high blood pressure and my restrictions. The classification was for my job assignment and living arrangements. And education was to make sure they had me there for the right class. I filled out so many I-60's for college that I had forgotten which class I was there for.

I was assigned as an SSI (i.e. Support Service Inmate) which is nothing but a janitor. At first, I was assigned to clean my dorm which was nice, because depending on which officer worked it would determine how much work I'd have to do that day. Some days would be awesome I could just sit at the table all day and watch TV or write letters. But other days I was working and cleaning everything in sight. Now there was a good side to this, once the officers saw that you would work and that you could be trusted. You would get some perks, like an extra tray at lunch time. It wasn't much but in prison, every little bit matters.

After about 2 months I was assigned to the Agg. Seg. Dorm and they were on lock-down 23 hours out of the day. And with this job you had to be quick and watchful. Because these inmates were the worst of the worst. They would throw any and everything at you, from spoiled milk to bodily fluids. And the officers depended on you to be alert.

But once the inmates saw that you were ok, it was a cake walk.

It's now Friday, and this is my first Islamic Service. The Friday service is called Jummah and the teaching class which was on Saturday is called Talim. Anyway, I get to service and the service goes on just fine. After services, I meet my new brothers and found out that I knew the leader from middle school. That gave me an edge, plus I was well versed in the teachings of Islam. So, I moved up the ladder rather quickly.

It was about 4 months later and I was voted in as the assistant leader of the Muslims. That meant that I had some pull on the unit, I was over one side of the unit and the leader was over the other. We were organized and disciplined, no one did anything without getting it okayed from the leaders. Now don't get me wrong, the leader and I would meet either at chow or on the rec. yard to discuss different issues.

We had to stay on top of things because if not the issues could quickly get out of hand. Issues such as if a brother got into it with someone who was affiliated with another group. Issues like this could cause race riots. So, to keep the peace, sit-downs were called on a regular basis. We would also come together to file grievances on the different officers who would try and stop us from performing our religious duties. We tried to stand for what was right, or at least what we thought was right.

Time seemed like it was going so fast, before I knew it the leader was going home and I was being voted in as the new leader. And by this time, I was no longer an SSI I was now working in the commissary. And I was living in the trustee area which was awesome, it was more freedom to move around and more relaxing. Some of the officers would even let us visit with one another. Life was good!

I was so into Islam that I was even getting a bit militant. Not in a racist way but in a religious way. I guess you could say I was one of those radical Muslims. The reason I say this, is because on 9/11 I stood in front of the tv and just clapped and cheered as the towers fell. I couldn't see it then, but it was one of the lowest points in my life.

Islam had changed me for the worst. I was putting hits (i.e. sending someone to beat up on another or worse) out on some of the brothers who needed a little discipline. But there was one thing that I would always wonder about, and it stayed at the back of my mind for the longest. It seemed like the people that were closest to me were all Christians, I mean we would eat together and watch movies together. And I never could understand that, I mean I would try to connect with my Muslim brothers but it never was the same.

Two years later God would begin to reveal why Christians and I were so close. On July 4, 2013, at 5:45 in the morning I was awakened from what I thought was just a dream, but it would turn out to be more than that. The dream was about me sitting in my grandfather's church in the front row like we did as kids, and I was listening to him preach. I popped up out of my sleep and just thought I was trippin because I was the Islamic leader and I had it made. So, I laid back down and tried to go back to sleep. And the dream came back only this time it was more convicting. So, I got up and started writing a letter to my grandfather and it seemed like the letter just flowed, I mean I must have written about four pages. I don't know what made me do it but I reread the letter and I was basically telling my grandfather that I was coming home, and not in a physical sense, but spiritual.

So, after the dream I tried my hardest to shake it. I would go to the chaplain's office to review tapes for Talim services, but I would go into the video closet and instead of looking at Islamic videos I would grab the Christian videos and watch them. I can remember watching a T.D. Jakes video and I could swear he was talking straight to me. He was saying stuff like, "you may be stuck with the decision of changing religions. You may be a Muslim right now, but you are searching your heart right now. You may be thinking about accepting Christ but you're scared." I was like are there any camera's in this closet?

I was convinced that I had to do some serious soul searching.

This went on for about two weeks, and I know God was in it because the officer who worked in the education department thought that I was one of his workers. But by this time, I was working for the Major of the unit as his SSI. Anyway, little did I know that God was moving on my behalf. So, I continued going to the education department and seeing the Chaplain. I did this for about two weeks and on July the 19th I called the Chaplain's Clerk into the closet and I asked him, "how do I accept Christ into my life?" As soon as the question left my mouth, the Chaplain's clerk began to rejoice. He told me that the church had been praying for me, ever since I was voted in as the Islamic leader.

They led me in the sinner's prayer and told me that they needed to lay hands on me and pray for the Holy Spirit to baptize me. I told them that I was not going to be fake and fall all over the floor and act like I had the Holy Spirit. I wanted everything to be for real. I said if it hits me it hits me. And nothing happened, but I knew there was something different.

I decided to attend one last Islamic service, as we entered in everyone was talking and laughing. But I was a little distant, I was trying to figure out how I was going to tell these brothers that I had excepted Christ. So, one of the brothers began to start the call to prayer and suddenly I just began to weep uncontrollably. I mean the type of weeping that you did when you were a little child, with the gasping for air and everything. So, I got up and went to the restroom and just tried to gather myself. But nothing was working!

Out of nowhere, some of the brothers came into the restroom and asked me what was going on and was I alright. I just simply told them that I was done, I was finished. And I just left and went back to my dorm. I began to gather up all my Islamic material and I just gave it all to one of the Muslim brothers. It was done, finally, I did it!

Now I knew what to expect! Because whenever you turn from Islam you become an apostate. And being and apostate means you must be punished. Yeah! Like a gang, blood in, blood out. But nothing happened, I went a whole weekend and nothing. I must be honest; I was scared out of my mind. But I wasn't mad, I knew they were only doing what they were taught.

So, Monday morning comes and I'm at work and I'm cleaning and suddenly one of the officer's approach me and tells me, "Jack!" I have to lock you up. I was like, "what?!" he then informs me that they found a note in the chow hall stating that there was a hit out on my life. They were going to shank me when I came to chow. I realized then that God was moving on my behalf. This time my Christianity was different and God was letting me know it.

I was locked up for about 7 days and finally the Major called me to his office. He was telling me that he was trying to find a place to send me. But Huntsville didn't want to move me and when he said that it was like a peace came over me. I just looked at him and told him, that's okay I'll be fine. So, I just turned around and went back to my cell and listened to my radio.

It was getting late and I decided I was going to go to sleep. But before I laid down I prayed. All I said was, "God, if it's Your will, I will face my enemies and go back out there to stand for You, but if it isn't Your will move me from this place. Send me to the Walls Unit, I know that a brother was sent there and

I can learn from him." After that, I just laid down and went to sleep.

I don't think I was asleep for more than 2 to 3 hours. And suddenly I heard a knock at my cell door. It was the officer letting me know that I was on the chain and that I needed to pack my stuff. I was blown away! So, I asked, "where am I going?" he told me that he didn't know just that I was being moved. I just began to weep because God heard me. He heard me!

Morning comes and I'm being escorted to the back gate to be put on the bus. I see that one of the nice offi- cers are working, so, I ask him where are they sending me. He grabs the paperwork and finds my name and he tells me that I'm going to the Huntsville

Unit, the Walls. I just start jumping and shouting and praising God for hearing my prayer. It was then that I knew, God had a purpose for me. And that my life would never be the same.

Chapter 7

ANSWERING THE CALL

The bus ride was long and we were packed in so tight that it wasn't funny. However, my mind was still blown away by the events that had just taken place. I'd never experienced my prayers being answered so fast. I mean I just prayed and left it in God's hands and He moved. That was all I could think about the whole ride.

I just couldn't believe how God was moving in my life. I would torture some of those Christians who thought they knew something. I would gladly debate them and if they weren't grounded in what they believed I would shake their very foundation. I'd bring up what Islam considered contradictions in the bible and most of the time that would end the debate. Or, I'd just out talk them.

I couldn't get my mind off everything that was happening. I was in outer space, it felt like I was the only one on the bus. All I can recall is when we were going through Houston to get to Huntsville. I was so excited to see my hometown, I stood up on the bus and got yelled at by the guards. I hadn't seen Houston in about 8 years, it had grown so much I barely recognized it.

When we finally arrived at the Wall's Unit and we entered the back gate, I understood the feeling that I had when I arrived at Torres Unit. I believe it was God telling me that my life was about to change, but at that time I was too blind to see it. But I was so happy that I'd gotten it now! It felt good to be able to be a brand-new person on a new unit. I was a new creation for real, my eyes were wide open and I was on fire.

The classification process at the Walls Unit was a little bit more organized. We were housed in the old gym of the unit. And there were no fields to go work in because the unit was in downtown Huntsville. Anyway, I remember we were going to the showers and I saw my friend BJ (a.k.a. Bryon Jackson) and I told him that I was assigned to the Unit and I asked him about his housing location. It felt so good, to see a familiar face, especially one that I knew was sound in his faith.

When we got back to our cells, I had the deepest need to pray. I mean God had been answering my prayers rather quickly. So, I got down on my knees, and asked God to move me to where BJ was. And I just rolled over and went to bed. I slept like a baby after I finished praying.

I received a lay-in for medical, education and classification the next day. Medical was the same as always, no change in my condition. But I found out God used the education department to get me moved. I was there for the Automotive trade. However, when I made it to classification, that's where God showed out. I was moved to the same cell block as my good friend BJ and our cells were right under each other.

When I finally finished moving and got settled into my cell, BJ came down and was inquiring as to what happened and why was I sent to the Walls Unit. I told him, "you might want to take a seat!" He got a little quiet and asked me what was going on. And without beating around the bush I just told him, "I've accepted Christ!" See you should understand something about BJ, he loves to joke around so he naturally thought I was playing. I told him, man I'm serious no joking around! He just jumped up and grabbed me and told me, "man it's about time!"

After that, I just gave him the run down on everything that had happened. I know he had to have been blown away, because I know I sure was. So, we just sat around and caught up on what all was going on. We were both just so excited about what God was doing now and in our individual lives. God was showing up and showing out!

The first church services I attended on the Wall's was on a Friday night. It was called New Birth and it was amazing. As a matter of fact, at the end of the service, Mr. Fisher who was the free world volunteer asked if there was anyone who would like to get up and give a brief testimony. I almost jumped out of my seat. So, I went up to the front and told them everything that happened to me. It was like I was so excited to brag on God because He was and is so worthy of His Praise. The things God was doing in me, were on a whole different level than I'd ever experienced before.

As the weeks moved on, I began to ask God to show me His truth from His word. I also asked Him, "What was the difference between Christianity and Islam?" About a few weeks later, God placed a hunger in me for His word that I can't explain. So, I started reading the bible from the very beginning and when I got to Genesis 15, God opened my eyes. You see, Islam base's its foundation on tracing its origin back to Ishmael the illegitimate son of Hagar the maidservant and Abraham. But from what I'd read, scripture said differently.

In Genesis chapters 15 thru 17, scripture clearly states that Isaac was the child of the Covenant and Ishmael was blessed on account of being Abraham's son. This alone confirmed everything for me, I was convinced beyond any shadow of a doubt that Islam was not the true way to God. And the same bible that I would kick around and try to disprove, I now believed it to be the infallible word of God. God began to minister to me in ways that I could never imagine. I've always heard that the word of God was alive and that His word would speak to you, but I never thought I would have ever experienced it.

God was opening doors left and right. I began to seek out the Chaplain on the unit every chance I had. His name was Chaplain Larry Hart and he had just gotten there a few months before I did. I still believe until this very day that God sent him over there just for me. I'll never forget our first conversation; I'd just told him my testimony and he looked at me and told me that just as Islam says that their religion is a way of life so is Christianity. That statement went straight to my spirit.

As time went on, God began to show me different things that at first I didn't understand. I would see all types of emotions in people's eyes. But I didn't understand it at first. One thing I did know, was to pray about everything, that I didn't understand. God lead me to go talk to Chaplain Hart and he counseled me on the Spiritual gifts of God and he told me that God had blessed me with a gift.

God also blessed me to be paired up with one of the boldest brothers I'd ever known. Brother Matthew Gonzales, he would stop and talk to anyone about Jesus no matter where he was. Chaplain Hart would call us the Bobbsey twins, because where you saw one, you would always see the other. And in prison, that was a rare thing to see, a black man and a Hispanic man hanging out together least of all calling each other brothers. Matthew taught me a lot, especially about the practical side of Christianity and how to operate in the gifts of the Spirit.

During this time the Lord gave me a vision and it was for underprivileged families and the youth. It's called C.H.A.N.C.E Ministries the sole purpose of this ministry is to awaken families to live a full life for Christ. This made me reflect on how I was raised and what my family tried to instill in me. Even though I missed it, I didn't want others to miss it. I would get bits and pieces of this vision and God would just tie it all together, all I had to do was write it down (Habakkuk. 2:2-3).

Years passed, and the fire was as strong as ever. God would place brothers in my path that would teach me so much. Some it was flat out, and other times it would be through experiences. But never the less it would be lessons well learned. Some of these lessons, at times would have me ready to pull my hair out. But God blessed me, I had Chaplain Hart, who was there for me on a regular basis.

I can remember this one session with Chaplain Hart, he had discerned from the Holy Spirit a prophetic message, that one day I would lead leaders, I was blown away. Chaplain Hart taught me so much! He taught me not just how to be a Christian man, but an all-around man. He would take his time and teach me things about manhood, the things that mattered most. He prepared me not just for the ministry but for my wife and my family too. He was not only my Chaplain, but he had become my spiritual father as well.

Doing my time on the Walls Unit was the most valuable experience of my life. The things I learned, no Seminary in the world could have taught. I learned humility in ways very few people get a chance to learn. I started out cleaning my Pastor's toilet and I was honored to do it. And I wasn't asked to do it, I asked to do it. I truly understood, that in all things do them unto the Lord.

After about three months, I was asked to be a door greeter. Now there is truly something very special about being a door greeter in prison. You get to be the first person in the church to love on everyone that comes through that door. You never know what a smile and a handshake will do. And in prison, that may just save a life!

God had me in what I considered a Christian boot camp phase for about a year. And within that year, God would move in my life in ways that absolutely blew my mind. After I finished my trade, I was given a job in the Mechanical Department as an Office clerk. I was working for the head of the department and he was something else. But Mr. Fisher who was over our Friday night bible study, also worked in this department. He saw that I was very frustrated about working for this man and he suggested that I pray for him. I began to pray for him and God gave me such a peace that I couldn't do anything but praise Him. The scriptures were coming to life, right before my very eyes.

As time moved on and God continued to minister to me, He also began to raise me up in the church. Like I said earlier, I started off cleaning toilets and then moved to door greeter. And now God was moving me to the choir, I knew it was God because I had no plans of joining the choir. It was during this time that I learned that God does things in seasons. And this was my season to be in the choir.

God used the choir to teach me about how important praise and worship was. At first, I thought the sole purpose of praise and worship was to honor God for who He is. Now don't get me wrong, that is true! However, in the Old Testament God also used praise and worship to defeat the Israelite's enemies. And He also allows us to use it to defeat our enemies.

Praise and worship for me helped me through some pretty tough spots. And by tough spots I mean TOUGH! I was so thankful for KSBJ 89.3 FM which is a Christian Contemporary Radio Station. I can remember they had this artist on and he made a very profound statement, he said, "our songs are our prayers that we get to share with the world." That statement made such an impact on me that I will never forget it.

Every job I had, I would make sure the radio was on KSBJ. I was getting job changes left and right. Most of them were from God, except for this one job. A friend of mine helped me get a job in the infirmary and this would turn out to be the worst mistake I could have ever made. And I mean the worst!

This wasn't the job for a growing Christian, the nurses were super friendly, and some of them were very attractive. They would make you feel like you were something, in the midst of a world that did their best to make you feel like you weren't anything. Needless to say, I got caught up! When you decide to feed the flesh, you'd better be prepared to pay the price.

During this phase of my walk, my flesh was weak as well water. I must have been in my 12th year of incarceration, so the attention of a woman was something special. To be honest with you, it melted me like butter. The nurses were friendly and very playful. As a matter of fact, they had the teasing game down. This took me all the way out of my Christian character, I was losing myself and I was fading fast.

I became such a hypocrite! I would put on the Christian face when my brothers came around, but when they left, it was back on! I was leading a double life, a life that I had turned over to God. I knew I was wrong and I was trying to back out of it. But it was hard, my spirit wanted to get right but my flesh fought me tooth and nail. It finally got to the point that I had to really buckle down and fast and pray.

I think I must have fasted for about a week! It was tough, but it was worth it. After the fast, I made it a point to go to church. During the service, God grabbed a hold of me and began to break me. I went to the alter and left everything there. I had to truly depend on God to get me out of the mess I had gotten myself into.

I thought the I was strong and could handle myself in a tough situation. But I was sadly mistaken. The enemy has a way of planting ideas in our heads to make us think like that. BUT GOD! Even in this situation, I learned a valuable lesson. And the lesson was, God will help us in any situation, if only we will give our problems to Him and repent.

After I'd repented, God began to move in ways that took my faith to new heights. First came a job change out of nowhere! I was moved from the Infirmary to the Craft Shop and that was a blessing. I was able to make money for myself and not have my mom send me her hard-earned money. Finally, after about 12 years, I could take care of myself. Things were finally looking up.

God sat me down for a little while from the ministry and that was the best thing. God's wisdom is so perfect in all that He does! And I'm speaking from hindsight. Because at the time that God sat me down I didn't under-stand it, to tell the truth, I was a bit upset about it! However, God's word is true and He does discipline those He loves and calls His own.

As I think about it, I believe I was sat down for about 18 months. I mean all I did was sing in the choir. Then suddenly, the parole rate picked up in our region and our choir director made parole. So, the Chaplain called him and me into his office and began to discuss the changes that needed to take place. I'll never forget it, Chap. looked at me and asked me was I ready. It brought tears to my eyes because I knew God was taking me off the shelf. I knew this because Chaplain Hart didn't do anything without being led by the Holy Spirit. So, he continued, "are you ready for leadership?" I looked at him and I took what he had asked me to heart.

So, I looked back at him, and looked directly into his eyes and told him that I was ready.

It's so wonderful to serve a God who forgives! I knew that God was in this appointment of leadership, because of how smooth the transition went. There was no envy being displayed nor jealousy amongst the brothers at all, I was welcomed with loving arms. This new phase of my Christian walk was very vital to my growth and I knew it.

As I started this new phase as Choir Director, God began to really minister to me. He began to show me the importance of praise and worship and how it applies to our lives now. God took me to the book of 2 Chronicles and showed me how singing and praise won battles.

In fact, it's in 2Ch 20:22 *"And when they began to sing and to praise, the LORD set ambushments against the children of Ammon, Moab, and mount Seir, which were come against Judah; and they were smitten."* This made me think about when my grandmothers use to sing or hum those old hymns in the kitchen. They were dealing with certain things in their lives and the only thing that gave them peace was praising God. So, I took this principle and taught it to the choir.

The Lord had placed it on my heart to teach the men that being in the choir was a very serious matter and one not to be taken lightly. There was no structure amongst the men, no personal responsibility in regards to being choir members. So, I went to Chaplain Hart and discussed what God was placing on my heart about teaching the men the importance of being in the choir. And he was all for it! I wanted them to know that being a choir member is a position that God honors and that they need to walk accordingly.

Now, there weren't any bad feelings towards me with the choir, and I believe that was because God gave me that position. But amongst each other, there was a little bad blood. Mainly because some of the brothers felt like they could do anything they wanted and get away with it. While the others were striving hard to walk as Christians. So, I began to put rules in place. Such as if you don't come to practice you don't participate. I did this because some thought they were irreplaceable and untouchable, so I had to get them to see that it's all about God and not about self.

Now I'm not going say that everything went smooth, because it didn't. Some of them said I was being too hard and others, well let's just say, they thought I had no clue as to what I was doing. But that's what happens when you're in leadership, you can't please everyone, you should just try and do what God leads you to do. And that's not always easy because it alienates you. And we as a people have a hard time dealing with being alienated from our peers, however, in leadership it's also a part of our pruning process.

It was getting close to my 15th year of incarceration and the Lord was introducing me to different aspects of leadership. I was now put over the Friday Night Bible Study it was called New Birth and this was a huge challenge. No longer was I over the choir and having to follow the Spirit in regards to songs, now it was about seeking the Lords direction for the teachings that He wanted to be taught. This required a new level of commitment to the Lord. I would have to try and spend as much time with Chaplain Hart as I could because I truly needed his guidance. I mean I was used to leading men in Islam, but that was all about the flesh. Leading men according to the Spirit is on a different plain.

Chaplain Hart taught me so much! He truly poured truth into my life. It's something how God will show you people and the roles that they are to take in your life. Chaplain Hart, took the role of spiritual father and that's the title he still holds in my life today.

I remember a time I allowed the wrong person to get up and speak. And I realized it from the time he opened his mouth. Anyway, word got back to Chaplain Hart and I was called to his office. He sat me down and before he even said a word I saw the disappointment in his eyes. That look alone broke me down and I began to weep. I wept because I'd never experienced a look like that from anyone who played such a huge role in my life. And for once in my life I cared about disappointing someone.

God had done a work in me that I never thought was possible. My view on life had totally changed and that was all God's doing. At this stage of my incarceration, I was just about to come back up for parole after completing six years of set-offs (i.e. being denied parole). And by this time, I was okay with the set-offs, because I knew I wasn't ready. After the third year of set-offs, I knew I wasn't ready. So, every parole visit after the third one, I would put in to go to Calvary Commission which was a Christian based mission's college. I did this because I knew I wasn't ready to be thrust back into a fast-paced society.

It was around the first week in September and I had received a lay-in to see parole, in fact, I was a month away from making my 15-year mark. It was the same as before nothing different at all. But I kind of felt like I had a good chance this time because I was almost done with my entire sentence. Three more years and I would be done. So, I left the parole visit and went to the chapel and just prayed. I had given it to God because He was the only one who really knew if I was ready or not.

As time went on, I just tried to stay focused on the things God had me doing and not worry about parole. Which was a hard thing to do, because I felt I was ready to live for God in the free-world. But I couldn't dwell on going home, I needed to trust God. So, I just stayed busy at the chapel and the craft shop. God had it!

Suddenly, after about six weeks I received a letter in the mail. And it was from parole! I was so nervous, I was shaking! All I could think about was, God, you know my heart! So, I finally built up the nerves to open it. And it was an FI-1! I just fell to my knees and praised God. Finally, I was getting out! But to what? Was I going home to mom or to Calvary Commission? Calvary Commission would be the best for me because it was more structured. But again, it was all in God's hands.

The next day I made a beeline to see my spiritual father, because we had to prepare for leadership change over. I thank God for Chaplain Hart because he taught me that a good leader always has his successor in mind from the beginning, and I did. So, Chap. and I decided that we would turn things over right away. As a leader, you have to discern when to step back. Because if you don't, you hinder yourself and others.

The very next day, I received a letter from Calvary Commission letting me know that they were looking forward to receiving me upon release. God had really taken care of everything, HE prepared the way for me. So, I just continued to prepare myself for getting out. I went to church and just listened to KSBJ on the radio. KSBJ really ministered to my spirit throughout my years on the Walls, they helped me through some tough times. Their theme is, "God Listens" and He does.

Time was flying, and now it was the end of November. I was getting nervous because in prison you kind of develop this hopelessness attitude and when it comes to parole that attitude is very strong. Reason being is because some guys have had their paroles taken from them. And that is a scary feeling. But I just kept pressing into God, because I knew it was the devil trying to get me to doubt God. But I wasn't falling for it, God has me forever and always.

It was November 29, 2010, and the officer that worked our wing, had just passed by for the 6 a.m. count time. About 20 minutes after that another ranking officer came to my cell and told me to pack my things, because I was getting out. I jumped out of my bunk and just thanked the good Lord. The whole cell block just erupted. There was so much yelling, that I couldn't understand a single word. All I knew was that they were extremely happy for me. Finally, it was over, the prison life was behind me and a new life before me.

Exiting those doors was kind of a bittersweet moment. I was sad and happy all at the same time. Sad because I was leaving some of my dearest friends behind, but happy because I was about to start a new phase of my life. As I was walking down the sidewalk lost in deep thought, I heard someone yell out my name. When I looked up I saw my Chaplain and Mr. Fisher standing there welcoming me back into society. The two men that poured so much into me for so many years, were standing with me at the most important time of my life.

I can't believe it took 15 years of incarceration to find the life I was meant to live. I was transformed from a misfit who cared about nothing and no one, to a minister of Jesus Christ. It's awesome how our testimonies are ongoing and how they don't end until the Lord calls us home. I am just so grateful that the Lord allowed me to tell phase one of mine.

ADDENDUM:

A God-Given Vision

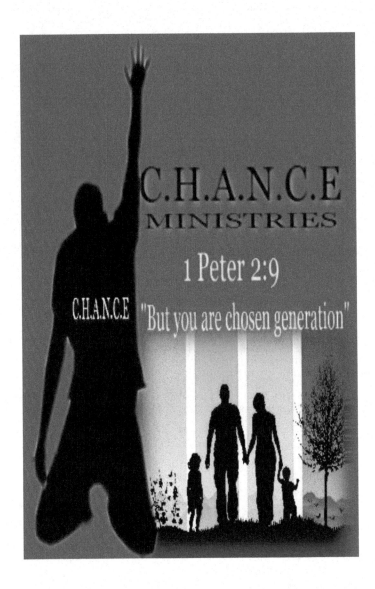

C.H.A.N.C.E.

Ministries

Reaching Families
In Our
Community

"If you have achieved any level of success, Pour it into someone else! Success is not success without a successor!

EST. September 3, 2006

By

Mr. & Mrs. Samuel & Tera Jackson

The Vision:

The **vision** of this ministry is targeted at supporting and encouraging those who have been denied the privilege of being granted with ***another chance*** in life. We want to assist our community in understanding that nothing is achieved without six basic skills that must be properly understood to be productive. Our ministry plans to assist those who have made bad choices into making better choices, by presenting them with the necessary tools to succeed.

This outreach presents the word "CHANCE" in the form of an acronym that stands for the following:

➤ **C**ommitment

➤ **H**onesty

- ➤ **A**ccountability
- ➤ **N**urturing
- ➤ **C**hallenging
- ➤ **E**ncouraging

The Plan:

The Plan of this ministry is to provide the proper understanding of what true ***commitment*** means and that it takes hard work to establish. We plan to show them that ***honesty*** is truly the best policy and that lying never gets you anywhere. This ministry wants to teach that ***accountability*** to God, self and to others helps to build strong character. By example, we will show them that ***nurturing*** is a vital tool when it comes to leadership. C.H.A.N.C.E. Ministries believes that by ***challenging*** them and them challenging themselves it will build confidence in their daily lives. And finally, we want to show them that by **_encouraging_** others it can also encourage them.

The Mission:

C.H.A.N.C.E. Ministries wants to provide the community with a strong sense of responsibility for the youth of today and the disadvantaged families they came from. intends C.H.A.N.C.E. Ministries goal is to show the world that all is not lost in regards to our youth and that giving up is not an option. This ministry plans on reaffirming them that with a solid foundation anything can be accomplished and that all it takes is a decision on their part.

C.H.A.N.C.E. Ministries stands on the scripture of, 1 Peter 2:9-10, **"But ye *are* a chosen generation, a royal priesthood, an holy nation, a peculiar people; that ye should shew forth the praises of him who hath called you out of darkness into his marvellous light: Which in time past *were* not a people, but *are* now the people of God: which had not obtained mercy, but now have obtained mercy."** Our youth of today have no identity. And they are our future professionals of tomorrow. And if we don't act now we may be in serious trouble, because who will be our doctors, lawyers, politicians, etc... If we refuse to take a stand for our youth today, our future is bound to cave in on us. And we want to remind the parents of their responsibilities in getting their children where they need to be in life.

C.H.A.N.C.E. Ministries hopes to educate the community on the awareness of the different diseases that are taking our country by storm. And what can be done to help prevent the continuous spread of such diseases! C.H.A.N.C.E. Ministries believes that the only way to save our communities is through direct communication with those who are placing themselves at risk of such diseases.

Prayer:

This ministries prayer is, to correct the mistakes that we've made in the past of not providing our youth with the needed information to make the proper choices in hopes of a better future, by providing them with the adequate education to make the proper choices for a better life.

~AMEN~

<u>UNITY</u>: *What Holds Us Together!*

A study based on the needs of
the Church...

&

Principles our families can use...

<u>Definitions</u>:

1. **<u>Love</u>:** (1) God (2) A deep, tender,
   ineffable feeling of affection and
   solicitude toward a person, such
   as that arising from kinship, rec-
   ognition of attractive qualities, or
   a sense of underlying oneness.
   [See 1Cor. 13:4-7]

2. **<u>Commitment</u>:** (6a) To make
   known the views of (oneself) on
   an issue. (b) To bind or obligate,
   as by a pledge. (commit) (1) To

do, perform. (2) To put in trust or charge; entrust.

3. **<u>Honesty</u>:** (1) Marked by or displaying integrity; upright. (2) Not deceptive or fraudulent; genuine. (3) Equitable; fair. (4a) Characterized by truth; not false. (b) Sincere; frank. (5a) Of good repute; respectable. (b) Without affectation; plain. (6) Virtuous; Chaste.

4. **<u>Accountability</u>:** (1) Liable to being called to account; answerable.

5. **<u>Nurturing</u>:** (1) To nourish; feed. (2) To educate; train. (3) To help grow or develop; cultivate.

6. **<u>Challenging</u>:** Calling for full use of one's abilities or resources in a difficult but stimulating effort.

7. <u>Encouraging</u>: (1) To inspire with hope, courage, or confidence; hearten. (2) To give support to; foster. (3) To stimulate; spur.

~BIBLE STUDY~

✠ **Love**:

John 13: 27-28 [God loves us despite what He knows of us]

Mark 12: 29-31 [The focus of all God's Laws]

Matt. 24: 12 [Difficult to love if you think only of yourself]

Luke 10: 27-37 [loving your neighbors]

John 13: 34 [Why loving others is so important]

John 15: 12, 13 [How do we love others as Christ loved us]

John 15:17 [Don't let small problems hinder you]

Rom. 5: 2 [Why it is key to the Christian life]

Rom. 12: 9, 10 [Real love takes effort]

✝ **Commitment**:

Gen. 22: 7, 8 [Learned through being tested]

Ex. 8: 25-29 [Don't compromise commitment to God]

2 Chr. 15: 14, 15 [God wants our total commitment]

Ps. 37: 4, 5 [How we commit everything to God]

John 12: 25 [What true commitment to Christ means]

Matt. 10; 38 [What it means to take up your cross and follow Jesus]

Acts 9: 15-16 [God calls us to commitment, not comfort]

1 Cor. 11: 3 [Submission is mutual]

✝ **Honesty**:

1 Sam 15: 13, 14 [Importance of... (Ps. 24:4; Pr. 19:1; Mic. 7:1-4)]

Gen. 27: 11, 12 [Proper motives for]

Ps. 6: 6 [Being honest with God]

John 13: 37, 38 [In estimate of ourselves]

✟ **Accountability**:

Judges 6: 13 [We are accountable for many of our problems]

Rom. 14: 10-12 [All are accountable to Christ]

✟ **Nurturing**:

John 4: 34 [Finding Spiritual nourishment]

~Spiritual Growth~

Gen. 12: 10 [Problems are an opportunity for]

Num. 33: 2 [Mapping your spiritual progress]

Deu. 5: 1 [Hearing, learning, and following]

Josh. 11: 18 [It is gradual, not instant]

Is. 58: 6-12 [Is shown by what we do and don't do]

Matt. 14: 23 [Time alone with God is important to]

Mark 4: 26-29 [Understanding the process of spiritual growth]

John 4: 13-15 [Parallels between physical & spiritual life]

John 15: 2-3 [God's pruning strengthens us]

John 17: 17 [How a person becomes pure & holy]

1 Thess. 5: 23 [Can't separate spiritual life from rest of life]

1 John 2: 12-14 [How we grow through life's stages]

✟ **Challenging**:

Josh. 1: 5 [Let God help you with life's challenges]

Neh. 2: 17, 18 [Challenging others with your vision]

2 Pet. 3: 18 [The world will challenge our faith]

✟ **Encouragement**:

Acts 14: 21, 22 [Giving it to new believers... (Philemon 1: 17-19)]

1 Tim. 4: 12-16 [Encourage others]

2 Tim. 1: 3 [Prayers can be a source of]

1 Thess. 5: 9-11 [Finding it from other faithful believers... (Heb. 12: 1)]

1 Thess. 5: 11-23 [We are instructed to be encouragers]

1 Peter 1: 3-6 [In knowing we have eternal life

Just a Thought...

Let us leave a legacy for our children
that we can be proud of. We need to
prepare the next generation for the
future so that they will have one.

CPSIA information can be obtained
at www.ICGtesting.com
Printed in the USA
LVOW06s2320100317
526833LV00002B/6/P